PRODUCTIVE HOMESCHOOLING

Our Unconventional, Accelerated, Debt-free, Values-centered Journey

PRODUCTIVE HOMESCHOOLING

Our Unconventional, Accelerated, Debt-free, Values-centered Journey

◦₰ THE CESPEDES FAMILY ₯◦

gatekeeper press
Where Authors are Family
Columbus, Ohio

Productive Homeschooling: Our Unconventional, Accelerated, Debt-free, Values-centered Journey

Published by Gatekeeper Press
2167 Stringtown Rd, Suite 109
Columbus, OH 43123-2989
www.GatekeeperPress.com

Copyright © 2019 by the Cespedes Family
All rights reserved. Neither this book, nor any parts within it may be sold or reproduced in any form or by any electronic or mechanical means, including information storage and retrieval systems without permission in writing from the author. The only exception is by a reviewer, who may quote short excerpts in a review.

The cover design, interior formatting, typesetting, and editorial work for this book are entirely the product of the author. Gatekeeper Press did not participate in and is not responsible for any aspect of these elements.

ISBN (paperback): 9781642377989
eISBN: 9781642377996
Library of Congress Number: 2019948745

CONTENTS

Dedication 9
How to Read This Book 11
Foreword 13

PART I

The Land of Opportunity 21
Our Education Left Us Wanting More 33
Building Our Family Foundation 44

PART II

Discovering Homeschooling 74
Securing Our Foundation 83
Our Homeschooling Adventure Begins 85
Homeschooling Regulations 97
Homeschooling Curriculum and Routine 103
Homeschooling Timeline 122
Our Surprise Blessing 132
Considering College and Alternatives 138
The Girls' College Experiences 149
Homeschooling Blessings and Benefits 164

Homeschooling Challenges and Pitfalls 170
Homeschooling is Not for Everyone 187
Transitioning from School to Work 192
Homeschooling's Greatest Gifts 202

A Final Message of Love to My Daughters 207
Great Quotes About Education 219
Resources 223
Tips for Assessing Homeschool Options 225
Appendix A 229
Appendix B 237
Appendix C 245
Appendix D 251
Appendix E 257
Appendix F 265

AUTHORS

Jan E. Cespedes
Vicki Cespedes
Ivana Cespedes
Belicia M. Cespedes
Briana G. Cespedes
Giana J. Cespedes
Eliana H. Cespedes

DEVELOPMENTAL EDITOR

Vivien Cooper

DEDICATION

To my loving wife, faithful partner, and steadfast rock, Vicki…
We did it, Mama!
We raised five beautiful, independent, passionate, Christ-following daughters who honor us with their life choices. Who would have thought you and I could have handled five daughters?!
What a state of immeasurable joy we have attained by being their parents. Training up our children in the way they should go has taught us many great lessons and strengthened our marriage!
Our little babies have grown into women with all manner of talents, abilities, smarts and giftedness. I know they couldn't have done it without their bright, caring Mama. Thank you, my darling, for loving our children and giving your life entirely to the uplifting of our family. Thank you for your faithful guardianship of their hearts and minds, as well as the supervision of their attitudes. (No grumpy hearts!) You were the greatest contribution to the heartwarming dynamic of our household.
I fell in love with the beautiful girl in the gym, not knowing that I had won a trophy. You are cherished amongst all other women. Your children rise up and bless you. You

THE CESPEDES FAMILY

have richly blessed my temporary moments on this earth as my crush, my girlfriend, and my wife.

As my body is overtaken with this aggressive cancer, I am praising Christ that you have been by my side through all the pain, suffering and defeat; successes and failures; joy, peace and victories of my earthly life. I know that many crowns await you in glory, Vicki.

We did it, Mama! We wrote our legacy. We finished the book!

Please know how much I appreciate the hard work you put into this project and the heart with which you wrote these words. May the following pages encourage many other mamas to educate, inspire and cherish their sons and daughters as much as you have, Vicki.

Your loving husband, admirer and partner in lifting high the name of Christ,

—Jan

HOW TO READ THIS BOOK

This book was written as a family legacy book, something very personal that would give our family (and hopefully others) over generations a peek into the home life and learning of this Cespedes family. It is the weaving together of seven narratives of personal memories and perspective into one story. Hence it will not read as an academic "how-to" book. But our hope is that you will glean some helpful nuggets from the personal testimonies shared.

Part I is exclusively family history, which will provide insight into our foundations and philosophy of education. However, if you are more interested in the homeschooling story itself, we suggest jumping to Part II.

Lastly, this book was written to offer grace, not guilt. We share the amazing things that have been accomplished to encourage you that such things are possible for a common, average family like ours. They are not to be taken as any kind of measuring stick of comparison. Your family will have its own unique and meaningful story. Do not allow the yoke of guilt to steal your joy and appreciation of it. Believe me, I

THE CESPEDES FAMILY

have struggled with this myself, and I know how suffocating the weight of guilt can be.

Take any nuggets you find helpful, use them, and toss the rest. And remember to share your story with others as well, including me. We are all in this together and we need each other.

On that note, we want to acknowledge the many people who may not be mentioned in this book but who were instrumental in our daughters' formation, education, discipleship, accomplishments, etc. From our little preschool co-op group, to our Life On Life friends, to teachers, tutors, pastors, older godly women, the girls' peers, various professionals, missionaries in our home, seniors who wrapped their love around them, etc. The list goes on and on. Thank you! This story would not be possible without you.

FOREWORD

Papa Jan

Now that four of our daughters are flourishing as remarkable adult women of character and accomplishment, we can say with confidence that homeschool worked for us. (Eliana is still very young.) Not only did homeschool work, it surpassed any expectations we would have dared to name at the outset.

Webster's Dictionary defines productive as "fertile, fruitful, high yielding; having a quality or power of producing, especially in abundance; effective in bringing about; yielding results, benefits and/or profits." This definition resonates with our experience. Ours has been an exceedingly productive homeschooling journey; a result beyond our dreams.

We, the Cespedes family, are writing this book to pass on to you, the reader, the many rewards, benefits, joys and blessings that have come to us from opting to give our children a homeschool education. We have undertaken the writing of this book as a family because that's how we have been blessed and impacted by our homeschool journey—as a family.

As you read through these pages, it is my hope that you will discover that homeschooling is more multi-faceted than

THE CESPEDES FAMILY

you could have imagined, and its benefits, rewards and joys much more abundant. I hope you start your own homeschooling adventure and discover how many places it can take you, and how productive it can be.

The idea for writing this book was first planted in my heart as a way to pay tribute to my wife, Virginia ("Vicki").

I thought to myself, *While I am still on earth to tell the world this story, I want the reader to know that homeschooling is the most desirable, most fulfilling and joyful occupation for a stay-at-home mama. If we can tell this story in book form, the entire world can read it, learn from it and most of all enjoy it! It's been such an amazing journey and I really want to share it...*

So, why do I say I want to tell this story while I am still on earth to tell it?

As I write this, I am sitting in a hotel room, recovering from radioactive iodine treatments for Stage IV cancer in the throat, chest, and lungs. I have just received the news that I also have degenerative changes of the spine as well as numerous bilateral pulmonary metastases that have slightly increased in size compared to my prior CT scan. (The largest is a 3.1 cm left perihilar mass which previously measured 2.8 cm.) So, as you can imagine, I feel a great sense of urgency in writing this book.

Little did my wife and I know how the blessings would continually flow when we first started our five girls (yep, that's right—five daughters!) in their homeschooling education.

My wife often thanks me for keeping her home so that she could have the opportunity to love, train and educate our daughters. She tells me that it is the most fulfilling job she could have ever had. The rewards of joy and love that she has received during this time would have never surfaced had she not made the sacrificial choice to stay home. Although she had many days of struggles and disappointments leading

PRODUCTIVE HOMESCHOOLING

these girls, it was all part of her formation as a wife and a mother.

Meanwhile, Vicki and I have started multiple businesses together—some good and some not so good. By starting these businesses together, we set an entrepreneurial example for our girls and demonstrated that it is about the effort you put in rather than the outcome of the business. We put in the work as we raised the girls and would not have done it any other way.

I am so proud of all of our daughters. Their collective accomplishments are a testament to the fact that homeschooling works and can avail much. I can't tell you how often Vicki and I are approached by people wanting to know how our daughters broke glass ceilings for age and education—accomplishments like the following:

- All four of our older girls graduated high school early, with Giana graduating the earliest at eleven years old;
- The girls were the youngest students at our local college (ages eleven to thirteen at the time);
- At age thirteen, Belicia was the top accounting student in college-level classes;
- At seventeen, Belicia was the youngest certified public accountant in the nation;
- Belicia was also recognized in the AICPA* list of 100 Most Influential People in Accounting [*the national organization of CPAs in America];
- All four of our daughters graduated college in different disciplines with completely different God-given gifts (except for Ellie, who is just eight years old);
- Each girl graduated no less than four years early with their bachelor's degree;
- Briana got her bachelor's degree at only fifteen years old;

THE CESPEDES FAMILY

- ☞ Despite her dyslexia, Giana was the youngest graduate at our local community college at age sixteen;
- ☞ Ivana—at sixteen, was the youngest certified nursing assistant at Pierce College;
- ☞ Belicia graduated with her master's degree at nineteen;
- ☞ Ivana graduated with her master's degree at twenty-one; and
- ☞ Ivana became a published contributor to a scientific journal at age twenty, for research she conducted while attending USC.

Not only are we incredibly proud of what our girls have accomplished, we are equally (if not more) proud of what wonderful human beings they have all become. They are not only impressive young ladies in terms of education and career accomplishments at early ages, they are also kind, pleasant and pure of heart.

This is no accident. Just as homeschooling has given us the luxury to nurture each of our daughters individually in terms of intellect and academics, so has it given us the luxury of nurturing the girls' individual hearts. Their collective integrity has been cultivated under the warmth, care and guidance of loving parents in their own home.

Perhaps one of the most obvious benefits of homeschooling is the cost-effectiveness—but it has proven to be only one of many blessings. It cost me but a smidgen compared to the high tuition necessary for private schools and college education these days. Back in 1984, I borrowed three thousand dollars from my mom to pay for my first semester at the University of Oregon while I waited for my football scholarship to kick in. Now it often costs ten times that amount per semester to attend that same public university.

In contrast, our daughters have been able to earn all their degrees and remain debt-free. This releases them from the additional financial burden carried by so many young adults and young families these days.

Above and beyond the incredible cost-effectiveness has been the peace of mind and reassurance I have gained from knowing that all my girls have been truly prepared and equipped with the solid foundation needed to walk out into an uncertain world and thrive.

It is my hope that as you settle in and turn these pages, or read this book piecemeal when you can find a few moments here and there, you will be able to glean the lessons from our story and save your own family's hard-earned money. More than that, it is my hope and prayer that you will discover as we did that homeschooling is filled with many gifts, blessings, rewards and wonderful surprises far beyond education itself. May you and yours be blessed as we have been all along the way.

Mama Vicki

You are about to read the story of a family made up of broken people, of clay pots. We are not a family that has it all together. We are a family with severely imperfect parents at its center—parents who were often on our knees crying out for wisdom because we didn't have a clue as to how to bring up the precious little souls God entrusted to us.

I made more mistakes than I'd like to admit. As much as I tried, I was not always in tune with the hearts of our daughters. (See Briana's entries.) I constantly questioned the whys and the hows of what we were doing. I daily felt that I was not doing enough, and the things I was doing were often not done well.

Most days I felt like a hot mess. If you had walked into our home on any given day, it would have looked like one too. Piles of laundry, stacks of dishes in the sink, little girls

THE CESPEDES FAMILY

in their pajamas with messy ponytails and dirty feet—these were the norm in our home, not the exception. Yet, as I write this and breathe in the sweet memories of those days, uncontrollable tears are streaming down my face.

It is hard to know where to begin in the sharing of this story but I am compelled to start by thanking God. After all, it was His goodness to us that made this story possible. He is the Sovereign One that ordained it and brought it to pass. He is the One that allowed Jan and I to have the parents, personal backgrounds and experiences that shaped our philosophies of education for our girls. And, He is the One that created each one of our precious daughters and gave to each one the daily capacities of curiosity, understanding and learning. He is the only one who could have made our homeschooling productive.

God is the One that transformed Jan and I as we grew in our knowledge of Him. We came to understand that we are sinners who have been saved by grace that only Jesus Christ can offer. So, we see our lives as a huge thank-you card to God. We are living a life motivated by thankfulness for all He is and all He has done for us.

While we can *never* repay Him, we continually seek to bring Him pleasure and to honor Him with every area of our lives. In the seeking, we have cried out to Him on a daily basis for the wisdom and knowledge of how to accomplish these ends. As it states in Proverbs 9:10, "The fear of the Lord is the beginning of wisdom, and knowledge of the Holy One is understanding."

—Jan (pronounced "yawn") and
Virginia ("Vicki") Cespedes,
parents of Ivana, Belicia, Briana, Giana
and our youngest, Eliana

Part 1

Meet Mama and Papa: What Influenced Our Philosophy of Education

THE LAND OF OPPORTUNITY

Mama Vicki

As I mentioned in the Foreword, it was Jan's parents and mine, as well as our personal backgrounds and experiences, that shaped our philosophies and paved the way for us to homeschool our daughters.

My mother, Bernardina Sandoval, and her mother were the first ones in their family to make it to the United States and become citizens. Once Mom got here, she was able to set up a home and life for us kids, however meager.

I was the firstborn in this country, and the youngest of three. Mom had done it—we were in America with a roof over our heads instead of a cardboard house. We had shoes on our feet without holes, and there was food on the table every day. We thought we were rich.

I remember the stories of the suffering and lack experienced by Mom's family back in Mexico. My grandmother, Maria Juvencia Reyes, grew up on a farm, washing her clothes in the river and taking care of her siblings. She had no edu-

THE CESPEDES FAMILY

cation at all. In the poor village of Jalisco, Mexico where she was raised, my grandmother had no prospect of education.

At the age of fifteen or sixteen, my grandmother (whom we called Tita) was at the river washing her clothes when a man on horseback kidnapped her and took her as his own. She felt that she had no say in the matter and the decision was out of her hands. This was simply the way things were and that was that.

When I was little, Tita would sometimes come and stay for months at a time to care for me. I have memories of her playing ball with me and cooking delicious meals for me—things like beans with cheese (which I love to this day), and quesadillas and fideo (Mexican noodle soup). She was always sweet and affectionate towards me and I adored her.

Tita was my safe place but she wasn't always safe herself. In fact, she was the one who started this migration to America, despite the danger and suffering it entailed. She endured so much, including an abusive husband, the loss of five of her children due to starvation, and long absences from her surviving children.

I cannot imagine being able to pick myself up and continuously fight against such difficulties and obstacles. Thankfully, she found the strength to do so and here we are today. Tita's story is a lesson in perseverance.

The Importance of Giving and Serving

Mama Vicki

I remember hearing stories about the differences between my grandmother's life and my mother's life. Mom was the eldest of nine children and one of the few to survive. Because of the realities of her life, she had to live with her grandparents and work on a farm. She was able to go all the way up to a second-grade education, an incredible achievement at the time.

Both Tita and my mom set their hearts and minds on creating a different and better life for their families. They were both determined to come to America, the land of opportunity, and come they did. It took many years and a lot of sacrifice. They were able to come to this country legally, and work as housecleaners in Southern California.

My mother was always willing to work hard, and to work with honesty and gratitude. She believed that she was entitled to nothing but had to work and earn the privilege of being in America, which she did. Although she undoubtedly would have qualified for government assistance, Mom never went on Welfare or food stamps. She never wanted to take advantage of the system that was offering her hope and a better life for her family.

Mom showed incredible tenacity, perseverance, and integrity in the way she lived. She was willing to climb over, go around, and deal with every obstacle before her, in order to bring to fruition her dreams for her children's future. She was never focused on herself but was instead motivated by the love she had for us kids.

I now realize that the most important things I learned in my early years came by way of my mother. I learned so much simply because of the person she was and the way she lived her life, prevailing over her painful and difficult upbringing.

My mother was generous and committed to her extended family. She taught us that even though we didn't have much ourselves, there was always something we could give. So, we took food and clothing to them. Mom also taught us to develop the habit of giving up some of our toys so we could give them to our cousins in Tijuana, Mexico.

THE CESPEDES FAMILY

One Christmas, Mom reminded me that God had blessed us with so much and that it was always good when we sacrificed for those in need. I had only my precious Raggedy Anne doll. So, I gave up my doll.

To this day, every time I see a Raggedy Ann doll, I remember my cousin's smile. This lesson in giving is something I was given by my mom, and something I passed on to my own girls. In the years to come, my own daughter, Ivana, would give up her Raggedy Ann doll for her friend in need. I will always be grateful to my mother for these lessons about giving and serving.

Education is a Gift

Mama Vicki

My mother exemplified grateful citizenry, excellent work ethic, genuine integrity, regard for God, and the pursuit of selfless dreams. She taught me, my sister, Maria, and my brother, John Joseph, the importance of living this way, day in and day out.

I was lucky to have great siblings. Maria was five years older than I and was like a second mom to me. She was smart, pretty, well organized, and very responsible. I looked up to her and still do. My brother John was three years older than I. He teased me and played pranks on me, like any normal big brother. He was also big, strong, handsome and quite intimidating (unless he was smiling his million-dollar smile). He was my protector, so the boys in elementary school stayed away from me.

Due to the age difference between us, my siblings and I didn't spend that much time together. They each had their own friends and went to different schools, and I remember feeling alone in my house most of the time. It felt like a normal experience rather than a bad one, and it worked out well for us. In hindsight, I wish I could have spent more time with my brother and sister. They are two of the most precious people in my life and I love them very much.

The dream of my mother was education. She believed that if you got an education, you could have a better life. She saw education as a gift rather than a right. I knew how much she had sacrificed in order to give us that gift and I didn't want to waste it. My amazing mom would eventually accomplish the difficult tasks of learning the English language, becoming a U.S. citizen, and earning her high school diploma at sixty-four years of age.

My mother's approach to life and education made a lifelong impression on me. Today, she continues to inspire me and teach me important life lessons.

Learning to Overcome Obstacles

Mama Vicki

My mother met my father here in the U.S. and I was the only child born in America. While Mom was trying to get residency in the United States, she was forced to leave my siblings in Mexico until she could earn enough to bring them here. Mom worked her heart out to get her residency and then brought Maria and John Joseph here as soon as she could.

My father denied paternity of me while my mother was pregnant and left her to fend for herself. So, Mom was a single mother. Once I was born, my father did see me and wanted to claim me as his own—but only on one condition.

THE CESPEDES FAMILY

He told my mother that he would marry her if she would send her two older children, my siblings, back to Mexico.

My mother refused, of course. When she did, my father's mother came to visit me and tried to kidnap me away from my mother. When my grandmother arrived, the babysitter called Mom. Since she worked right across the street, Mom was able to come right over, and prevented the kidnapping. Afterward, Mom put a restraining order on my father to keep him away from me. So, I never knew him.

I grew up in impoverished, gang-infested neighborhoods deep in Los Angeles. That was all we could afford. I had no idea our neighborhood was unsafe. To me, it was simply home.

My mother had to work two jobs in order to provide for us. This took up so much of her time, she wasn't able to be as involved in our lives as she wanted to be. I was a latch-key kid. Although working so much prevented Mom from attending our school events, accompanying us to play dates and attending PTA meetings, she still found time to give us wonderful and meaningful childhood memories. She made sure we knew how fervently she loved us and how much she supported us.

In elementary school, I was an obedient, compliant kid who did everything I was asked to do and avoided getting into trouble. This made some kids really dislike me. They often called me teacher's pet and other equally hurtful names. I remained extremely quiet, to the point where teachers often reached out to my mom to make sure that my quietness wasn't a symptom of an issue that needed to be addressed.

I was also the tallest person in my entire school until I was eleven years old. So, on top of being called teacher's pet and other names related to being quiet and compliant, I was often called Twin Towers or Statue of Liberty.

From my very earliest years, I believed that even hard things were good. I had a simple understanding that these biblical words were true: "And we know that God causes all things to work together for good to those who love God…" (Romans 8:28)

I believed that even hard things were good.

This belief I had carried with me since childhood—that even challenges and obstacles were good—would become something I could pass along to my own daughters. Knowing this enabled me to instill in our girls the ability to face and overcome challenges they would face in education and in life. It would prove to be a great blessing and comfort as we all lived with the impact of Jan's ongoing illness.

We sought to teach our girls by example. This calls to mind a great quote by Albert Einstein: "Example isn't another way to teach; it is the only way to teach."

THE CESPEDES FAMILY

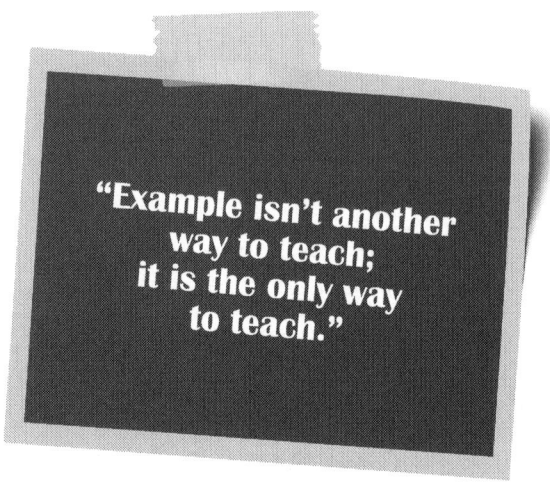

"Example isn't another way to teach; it is the only way to teach."

Discovering My Likes and Dislikes

Mama Vicki

My elementary school teachers saw a real brightness in me and encouraged me academically. I was often recognized academically and, thanks to my work ethic in the classroom, I was given special privileges reserved for honors students. I started to latch onto that identity.

For junior high school, I was accepted to Pacoima Junior High Theatre Arts Magnet Program, an honors program in our community. I discovered a love for music and dance and also started to take drama classes, which were painful because of my extreme shyness. Ultimately, drama classes helped me come out of my shell—so much so that, by eighth grade, I had the lead role in our junior high's production of the musical, *Bye Bye Birdie*.

Resisting my impulse to stay in the background, I entered Shakespeare competitions as a solo actress and won first place. It was so hard for me to do full monologues; somehow, I pulled it off.

Junior high was filled with drama of all kinds. I enjoyed drama class but didn't like the drama that went on outside of the classroom. It was a season of life where things seemed trivial and silly, especially in the way kids would try to relate to each other and the experiences they wanted to have.

Sometimes girls became possessive of their friends, and the atmosphere wasn't conducive to healthy friendships and relationships. Girls were often upset with me because I had inadvertently drawn the attention of a boy they liked. Even sleepover pajama parties became dangerous; girls who were only eleven, twelve, or thirteen stole liquor, smoked and accidentally lit things on fire. It was all very uncomfortable, so I usually declined these invitations.

Despite the various challenges, I excelled in junior high school academically, and carried my love for dance and music into the rest of my life.

A Born Athlete

Papa Jan

I grew up in the San Fernando Valley region of Southern California and spoke Spanish exclusively. My parents, Henry and Isabel Cespedes, were recent immigrants from Cuba. They had lost everything in the Castro revolution. My dad came from a wealthy family in Cuba—one with a rich heritage—so these losses were substantial.

THE CESPEDES FAMILY

My great-great-great-granduncle is called the Padre de la Patria (the Father of the Republic) and started a revolution against an oppressive Spanish regime. He was named the first president of the first democratic Republic of Cuba. His likeness appears on the ten peso bill. His statue and monument still stand in the Capitol of Havana, Cuba, and there are streets and parks named after him, as well.

When my parents came to the United States, they had to start from nothing, leaving family behind. My father worked very hard, carrying three jobs, managing Jessup Farms, and eventually starting his own business, Henry's Tree Service.

Meanwhile, Mom went back to school to earn her teaching credential, as well as a Master's Degree, and became a full-time teacher and counselor for LAUSD. They started having their own kids—my sister, Elvia, my brother, Eric, and me—and brought many family members to America, as well. I am named after a very dear friend of my dad's named Jan Von Engel—the man who helped my father start a new life here in the States.

I loved my wonderful Cuban upbringing, filled with family, Cuban parties, and great food. At the same time, my Cuban heritage meant that Spanish was my primary language, and this made it difficult for me to transition into English. This was compounded by my dyslexia—a condition I didn't know I had until my daughter Giana was diagnosed forty-six years later.

PRODUCTIVE HOMESCHOOLING

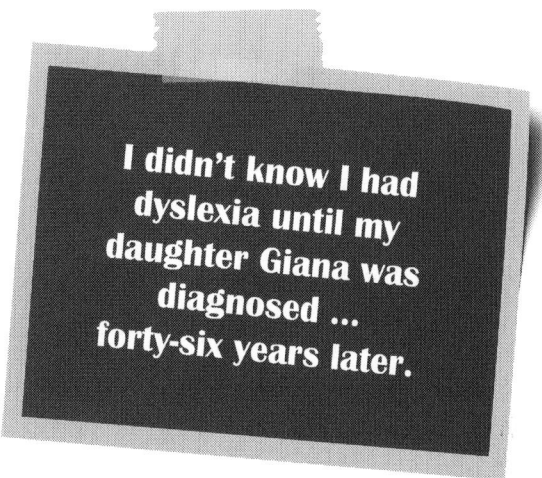

I didn't know I had dyslexia until my daughter Giana was diagnosed ... forty-six years later.

I must have inherited dyslexia from my dad, who was formally educated at Cal Poly San Luis Obispo in the States and yet struggled with pen and paper. Mom on the other hand was a wiz—a straight-A student. No wonder my sister is so smart and professional. Fortunately, I also inherited my dad's athletic skills. Sport became my focal point at school and I spent every minute of my free time playing in the park with my buddies.

I began my formal education at a Baptist elementary school in Panorama City, California. I was an average student, no doubt because my English was very poor. After completing elementary school, I attended Robert Fulton Junior High, a very large public school in Van Nuys, California. I did well because the curriculum was easy and I put in the effort to study and do my work. I was a good boy in school because that is what I was taught to be. I quickly became the athlete of the school, so I was popular, especially among the girls.

For high school, I attended Saint Genevieve in Panorama City, California—a private parochial school. I was an average student, due to the amount of schoolwork and the curric-

THE CESPEDES FAMILY

ulum demands. I did all the work to the best of my ability, but ultimately prioritized sports. During that time, I was also working for my dad, climbing trees, cutting grass and driving trucks.

    Mr. Rudy Trujillo, Vice Principal of the school, was my spiritual and academic counselor. He helped me make sense of people and problems, and helped me recognize my potential. We are still friends to this day and we enjoy a game of racquetball now and again. He continues to be a great mentor in my life.

    My basic philosophy during school was this: sit in the back, be quiet during class, do the homework and study for the exams—if and when I had time. This worked out well enough for me, as I ended up graduating with a 3.0 GPA. Clearly, academics was not my priority.

    The disadvantages inherent in this mindset are so vivid to me now. As we went on to educate our girls in our home, we prioritized not just proficiency of the subjects but an earnest love for learning. Vicki and I both know the value of a genuine love for learning, and hoped to instill the same love in our girls. We knew that ongoing learning would serve them well in all aspects of adult life, and we didn't want them to miss out on such a gift.

OUR EDUCATION LEFT US WANTING MORE

Uninspired by High School

Mama Vicki

For high school, I was accepted into the Theatre Arts Magnet Program at Hollywood High School. Knowing that the program was considered special and elite, I felt it would be wrong to decline to go. I entered high school excited. I was expecting to find the academic ardor higher and the classwork more challenging.

Unfortunately, I was quickly disappointed. I discovered that the academic standard they set for students was shockingly low. High school seemed to be a repeat of junior high, with a few more electives. I was disappointed and knew that I would need to transfer to a different school. I was planning to go to college and knew that I was going to need the proper academic training in order to be fully prepared. I needed something more challenging.

THE CESPEDES FAMILY

In my junior year, I transferred to St. Genevieve—a much better match for me. The school had a reputation for being rigorously academic. It was indeed more challenging.

Again, the high school drama continued, with plenty of cliques, gossip and trivialities that seemed to me to have nothing to do with serious academic learning. It wasn't that I felt superior to anyone, it's just that I was in school for one reason: I really had a hunger to learn. I didn't enjoy the party atmosphere, all the experimentation, or the constant jumping from one relationship to another.

PRODUCTIVE HOMESCHOOLING

Letting Opportunity Chart My Course

Mama Vicki

When it was time to submit my college applications, my high school counselor encouraged me to apply to my dream schools. So that's what I did. I applied to Harvard, Yale, Princeton, UCLA, Oxford, Cambridge, etc.

When I received acceptance letters to all these schools, I was shocked and conflicted. I knew I couldn't leave my mother. She was going through a very difficult time in her marriage and it was heading toward divorce. Given everything Mom was going through, I was not about to add to her already heavy burden. I felt that I had to stay and be there for her.

Mom had sacrificed so much for us kids for so many years. I knew I could never repay her but the least I could do was make her life a little bit easier by staying home and attending college locally. I decided that the best and only viable option for me at that time was to stay home and find a local college I could pay for with money I earned.

I enrolled in California State University Northridge (CSUN) and took community college courses. I did this for two years, focusing on getting all of my general education courses out of the way. I was undecided as to the direction I wanted to take in my studies, and didn't yet have a sense about my true gifts and aptitudes. I knew that I could study, do well on tests and get good grades—but I was all too aware that I knew little that would be truly useful in any career or income-producing endeavor.

After two years, Mom's divorce became final. I still wanted to stay close to her, so I decided to transfer to UCLA, where I was offered a full academic scholarship. I chose to major in Communication Studies because I wasn't sure what else to do. UCLA was known for their communication studies department so it seemed like a good choice.

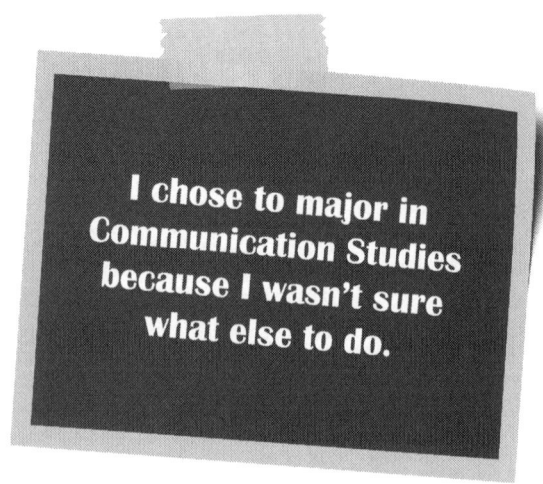

PRODUCTIVE HOMESCHOOLING

I was very successful at UCLA and maintained a 4.0 GPA. I was active in every honors society available to me, started and created several organizations on campus, and often served as president for the organizations of which I was a part. And yet, I felt like I was wearing a mask. People considered me very intelligent, but I didn't *feel* intelligent in the same way that people perceived me to be. I felt like I was primarily good at taking tests.

I wanted so badly to learn and acquire tangible skills that I could use to benefit society and generate an income to help provide for my mom. I knew that no one would pay me to be a professional student—and yet being a student and doing well on tests was the only skill I felt sure that I had.

These were the primary skills I had acquired in school: being able to memorize facts, spit them out during an exam, and get a good grade. I couldn't think of a single career that utilized those skills. I knew that, if I was going to enter the work force, I needed to be able to actually *do* something—not just remember things I had been taught.

Without any real direction, I had done the only thing I knew I was good at—I continued on in school, pursuing my bachelor's degree, then my master's degree, and ultimately my doctorate degree.

After finishing my bachelor's degree, I was offered a full scholarship for a master's program at UCLA in educational psychology. Naturally I took it. I was so grateful for the opportunity to be educated for free. It was really the opportunity determining my direction, and not my own thought-out decision coming from the passions of my heart.

When I was offered a scholarship to start my Ph.D. program in educational psychology, I just followed. I said, "I guess this is what I am supposed to do next."

> "I guess this is what I'm supposed to do next."

I was very confused by psychology. There were many different approaches, everything was relative, and there was no way of knowing what was actually right and true. Then I took a statistics course and realized that I could manipulate my research depending on what statistical method I chose to use. I found myself asking, *So, what is true?*

> It bothered me to think that all the research and all the written material I had been studying that was supposed to inform my reality was nothing more than one person's manipulation of data.

I started questioning my goals and asking myself what I was trying to accomplish, exactly. I wondered, *Am I just studying in order to complete what I started and make my mom proud?*

Even though I had these nagging doubts inside me, I tried to make the most of my education and I succeeded. I was able to gain advanced degrees and always seemed to be at the top of my class. I was afforded good opportunities and had wonderful teachers and enriching experiences.

I was blessed by these good opportunities and teachers who did their very best to invest in us students and make a real difference in our lives. Overall, the public-school system was kind to me and I am thankful for the experience. At the same time, I couldn't help but wonder if I had missed something.

Unprepared for Life

Mama Vicki

Jan and I grew up with the tremendous privilege of public education, and we have always been grateful for it. We were blessed to have been educated in the United States of America, not in an impoverished country or one torn apart by Communism. When it is hard for an average family to afford an education, the kids often stay home without instruction or begin working very young. Many end up on the streets and make unwise choices while they're young that carry lifetime consequences.

We had access to free education for thirteen years of our lives, beginning with kindergarten. It was an amazing gift, and one we did not take lightly. We mostly had good teachers who really cared about us and wanted to help us succeed in this world. So, I have always had a deep respect and admiration for teachers who invest their lives for the good of others.

THE CESPEDES FAMILY

I learned many things during my thirteen years in the school system. Yet, once I had graduated, I came out feeling inept, unskilled and unprepared for life as an adult and a responsible citizen. I was an eighteen-year-old with no ideas for my future career and no direction for my life. I wasn't aware of any skills I possessed that I could use to generate an income.

I didn't have the skills to manage my finances, enter into a healthy marriage relationship, or properly feed, raise and care for my future children. Forget about starting or running a business. That seemed completely out of reach.

I said to myself, *Well, now I am a college-educated adult. But I didn't get any courses on how to live my life in a way that is wise, productive and useful to society. There weren't any courses to help me assess and explore my unique capacities, passions, and mission in life. Why weren't there any courses to prepare me for the work force by the time I was sixteen years old and eligible for a work permit? Why wasn't I taught specific skills I could develop sufficiently to become gainfully employed?*

Overcoming My Learning Disability

Papa Jan

Because of my learning disability, it was hard for me to read at an accelerated level and write well, which college demands. I struggled through pages at a time. If I didn't intentionally focus and push myself beyond my comfort zone, I fell behind. The services and resources that people with learning disabilities receive nowadays were not accessible to me back then. So, I just had to pull myself up by my bootstraps and move forward. (My daughter Giana grapples with this same condition. I am proud that she finds ways to motivate herself, just as I did, even when she feels incapacitated.)

PRODUCTIVE HOMESCHOOLING

Now I am an avid reader, and I read a range of books, from theology to historical biographies to current political arguments. When someone first walks into my house and looks to the left, they see two large bookcases, full of classic literature. We used these books as part of the homeschool curriculum for the girls. Beside each of the four desks in the house there were two more bookcases, brimming with books. Eventually we designated an entire room as the family library.

It may be because I wrestled with reading and with English in particular that I became so motivated to teach my girls to become devoted readers, dedicated to learning everything the pages of a book could teach them.

The rest of my education really played a role in the formation of my own philosophies toward it. I was able to go to the University of Guadalajara in Mexico where I studied Mexican Revolutionary History. I also attended Cal State Los Angeles to take some business classes, where I did very well, largely due to my business interest. I was eager to learn and found my wheelhouse in these classes.

Facing Political Bias

Papa Jan

After high school, I earned a full-ride football scholarship to the University of Oregon. Again, I was an average student in the political science department because my focus was football. I was very interested in geopolitical studies in Latin America, especially the Iran-Contra affair in El Salvador. Being the son of immigrant parents from Cuba, I have always felt extremely passionate about Latin American politics.

THE CESPEDES FAMILY

For four years, I struggled through the overwhelming, politically-charged campus environment. I was very discouraged with the liberal bias obvious in every professor and every classroom curriculum. Every subject was full of political undertones; it pushed me further to conservative viewpoints.

A couple of college stories are perfect examples of this. One day a speaker came to one of my classes promoting Fidel Castro's communist revolution and his progressive accomplishments.

The minute the speaker started talking, my blood began boiling. I felt a strong urge to say something. So, I spoke up and stated that the socialist regime Castro had promised was anything but harmless. With a heated intensity, I explained that Castro has turned the Cuban government into a tyrannical state, making it the poorest country in the western hemisphere.

When the speaker asked me if I knew any pre-Castro history, I responded with a number of facts concerning the Batista regime and the value of the Cuban peso prior to Castro's dismantling of the economy.

When he disregarded much of my argument, despite its obvious merits, I found it infuriating!

In another instance, I was in a Russian geopolitics class and learned that, during the Russian Revolution of 1917, the people rose up to reform Russia because the Czar had become tyrannical. Over a period of three class sessions, our professor listed every political leader that the Communist Party executed in order to gain power.

I began to understand the means by which the Communist Party rose up. It was incredibly sad to hear of all this death and destruction. I looked over at my fellow classmates to see if they shared my alarm.

Once again, I felt like I needed to say something. So, I spoke up and talked about Castro's tyrannical dictatorship.

And once again, the professor responded with something along the lines of, "Just as the Russian Revolution turned into a communist empire, Castro turned Cuba's revolution into a communist empire that may one day engulf all of Central America and the Caribbean."

Without thinking, I piped up and said, "That's stupid. The only way he could do that is through mass murder!"

My professor replied, "In order to improve the state of countries, sometimes the blood of patriots must be shed."

I was fuming with anger. Not only had he taken this powerful Thomas Jefferson quote out of context, he had redefined the actions and purpose of actual patriots—people who support their country at all costs for its good. There is a huge difference between those who fought for what was best for them and those who fought for what was best for their people. Throughout history this difference is clear and a matter of common sense to us as moral human beings.

I was so aggravated by the professor's teaching that day, I walked out of the class and didn't return back until the final. I ended up getting a C- in that class and didn't care a hoot.

I was very outnumbered in the values and principles I held at that school, and I can only imagine what conservative kids have to endure on college campuses these days. I received C's in most of my political classes other than my Latin American studies. I left the University of Oregon with a 2.60 GPA and this thought: *What a waste of time!*

BUILDING OUR FAMILY FOUNDATION

Love, Marriage, Work

Mama Vicki

Jan and I grew up only a few miles from each other, but we didn't meet until 1985. I was sixteen years old and attending Jan's alma mater, St. Genevieve High School, where I was on the cheerleading squad. He was twenty at the time and in college.

He was the star athlete of St. Genevieve High and had gone on to play college football at the University of Oregon. He was very popular in our community and many girls had a crush on him. I, on the other hand, was a quiet girl, focused on my studies and determined to do well in school. I did not date and had not yet had a boyfriend.

Jan came home from college for the summers. One summer he was coaching the new St. Genevieve quarterback, Dion, who happened to be a good friend of mine. Dion asked me to stay after cheerleading practice to meet a friend of his. To my surprise, it ended up being the popular local hero, Jan Cespedes.

After a brief meeting, Jan was bold enough to ask for my home number.

He seemed like a nice guy but I opted not to give him my number. I didn't give my phone number to people I had just met. It would take me a long time to let myself trust him.

Over time, I saw that he was a good guy who loved God and was respectful and patient with me. Our relationship grew slowly but surely.

It was Jan's commitment to God that made me fall in love with him. As our relationship grew, he taught me about God, taught me to pray, and led me to sound churches where I heard the gospel of Jesus clearly preached and lived out. Jan was instrumental in the blossoming of my Christian faith.

Over time, I found many other reasons to love him, as well. His joy was irresistible, as well as his kindness to everyone, especially children and the elderly. Then there was his humor, his great big smile, his baby-blue eyes, his love for his family, and his deep and loyal love for me, which came as a real surprise.

In 1992, Jan proposed at a church that he helped to build in Tijuana, Mexico and, in 1993, we were married in that very church.

Papa Jan

After I finished my football adventures at the University of Oregon and graduated with my B.A. in Political Science, I was invited onto the coaching staff as a graduate assistant coach for kickers and receivers. This was enjoyable, kept me in the game, and afforded me the perfect opportunity to continue to train and try out for NFL teams. Unfortunately, I was quickly and rudely awakened to the reality that the success I achieved in collegiate football was not of NFL caliber.

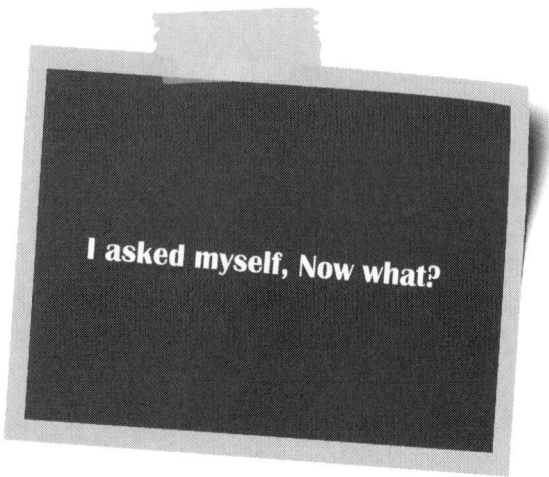

I asked myself, Now what?

I loved football and knew that it was my natural God-given fit. Ultimately, the stronger tugging of my heart was leading me to serve my church and get to know God. So, I returned home, received counsel from my local parish and thereafter signed up to serve abroad as a Christian missionary.

I joined the Salesians' priest candidacy program. This journey would entail two years of living in a Salesian community with other missionaries from all over the world. It was a great two years, serving the local community, building a church and, of course, organizing sports programs for the kids. During my time in the Salesian priest candidacy program, I followed a program of study, ministry and prayer. I lived with three priests for those two years, made many friends and had a few girlfriends. The vow of celibacy was not in the cards for me.

I knew I was doing good works—working with youth, running sports camps, helping to build houses—but it was secular in nature and not fulfilling enough for me. I wasn't ministering to people at the heart level, sharing the gospel or helping people to love God more.

So, I moved back to the States and got a job at St. Francis High School in La Canada, California, teaching Spanish and coaching football. I also reignited a high-school sweetheart relationship with Vicki, the accomplished girl who would become my wife.

During our time apart, she had always been in my mind and heart. I had kept a picture of her with me for all those years and I wasn't willing to give up hope. As I taught Spanish and coached football, we finally dated and I fell deeply in love with her. I decided that Vicki was the one for me so I proposed.

She said yes. In August of 1993, we married at the church I helped build in Tijuana, Mexico. Father Romero—the priest I served for in the candidacy program—married us. It was so meaningful to have him be the one to officiate at our wedding.

By the following summer, it had become clear that my teacher's salary wasn't going to cut it now that I was a married man and about to start a family. I realized that I needed to put my name out there and get back into the business world. Thankfully, the hand of God was on my situation.

During my last year of teaching and coaching football, I took an interest in a student who was struggling. His father happened to be a wonderful man named Charlie Frankowski, the President of Kelly Clark Food Brokerage. He hired me as a salesperson and with that job, Vicki and I were able to buy our first home in Los Angeles.

God's Grace

Mama Vicki

When I got the feeling that I had missed something as I completed my education, I was sensing the guidance of God. I began to realize that I had indeed missed something.

THE CESPEDES FAMILY

During the writing of my dissertation, I was having trouble putting my dissertation committee together. At that time, I thought of myself as a devoted Catholic Christian and wanted to study the role of faith in the counseling room. Because of the religious nature of my topic, my immediate mentors were not interested. So, I had to go outside UCLA to find someone who would be willing to sit on my committee.

Then Jan heard on the radio that Dr. John MacArthur and Dr. Jay Adams would be speaking on Biblical counseling in a local Calvary church. Dr. MacArthur is the pastor of Grace Community Church, and is considered one of the finest expository preachers of our day. He is also a prolific author. He is known for his faith and is bold in his exaltation of God and His word. Dr. Adams is known for his foundational study and book on the topic of Biblical Counseling-Nouthetic Counseling (defined as a form of Evangelical Protestant pastoral counseling, based solely on the Bible and focused on Christ.)

Jan and I attended the talk and that night, I discovered what I had been missing: Christ. I know it may sound odd to say that I was a Catholic Christian but was missing Christ. Allow me to explain. As a Catholic Christian, I had a *religion* but not a *relationship* with my savior. I believed in God but trusted in my own good works for salvation. I was all about the do's of my Catholic faith, and was trying to earn my way into Heaven.

> I had a religion but not a relationship.

When I became a Christian, I realized that I could never be good enough—but the good news was that I didn't have to be. Salvation is a free gift from God. It is given by grace, not earned by works. As it states in Ephesians 2:8-9: "For it is by grace you have been saved, through faith—and this is not from yourselves, it is the gift of God—not by works, so that no one can boast."

I was overwhelmed when I realized that I could not save myself but Christ had done it for me. I thought to myself, *This is undeserved forgiveness and salvation!*

It was the most precious gift I could have ever dreamed of receiving—God's forgiveness of a sinner like me, someone who thought they could be good enough to earn Heaven. Now, He resides in my heart and I love Him. I learned that Christ is the only source of truth, and my soul was hungry for it. That night, He began to transform the life of a sinner to a woman that was saved by grace.

Hearing their talk at the church lit a fire inside me. I felt a burning desire to live my life in a way that pleased God and was centered around others. Suddenly, my life had purpose, direction, and meaning. Now it was time to learn, to soak my mind and soul in truth, and then apply what I learned to my everyday life and all my relationships. After all, isn't that the goal of learning?

I felt like I had to start from scratch, and I found the idea refreshing. I felt like I had to learn my role as a woman, a wife and a homemaker. My life was exciting and, for the first time ever, it was clear and deeply fulfilling.

Papa Jan

Our love for Christ and our desire to grow spiritually led us to start attending different churches, including Lake Congregational Church in Pasadena and the Nazarene Church with one of our favorite authors, Dr. Jay Adams.

Having been granted a saving relationship with God changed everything. Vicki and I were deeply interested in truth and sincerity, not religiosity and liturgy. We were full of passion for Christ and hungry to learn about God. We wanted to study His word and dig deep into knowing God and living the way He wanted us to. In fact, it was our mutual enthusiasm for truth that became a large factor in our decision to homeschool our girls and educate them with a Biblical worldview.

As our walk with God became the most important endeavor of our lives, we realized how little we actually knew. It became clear to us both how much we needed to invest time, resources and energy into the study of God and His word.

I decided to enroll in seminary. I knew that the workload would be weighty and intensive, and I would need time to take all the classes and do all my coursework. So, I quit my great sales job and we moved to North Hollywood, which was close to the seminary I attended.

PRODUCTIVE HOMESCHOOLING

Preparing for Parenthood

Mama Vicki

On one very happy day, Jan and I found out that we were pregnant. To be honest, for most of my life up to that point, I hadn't given much thought to having children. I knew that the gift of parenthood came with tremendous responsibility and weight, and I found it sobering. I didn't know the first thing about walking through pregnancy, and even less about parenting a child.

I set my heart to start learning. I searched the Scriptures, read every book I could put my hands on, and asked questions of all the exemplary parents I knew. I really wanted my children's upbringing and education to be different than mine—and yet I couldn't envision an alternative to the conventional, institutional paradigm.

As a new believer, I'd had a complete shift in my heart's desires, my motivations and the purpose of my life. I now wanted to pour my life into those things that He was asking me to do in the Bible, and I became willing to do anything I could to please Him. I felt that it was the least I could do for such amazing forgiveness and love.

I started to look more closely at my role as a wife. I was reminded once again that I was sorely unprepared to run my own home. I didn't know how to cook, organize or budget. I dedicated myself to learning and then applying to our marriage what I had learned. I took all the courses I could get my hands on and asked godly wives for help and wisdom. I set my heart on being the best wife I could for Jan and I have to say, he offered me a great deal of patience and grace. He still does.

For the first time in my life, I felt true joy and fulfillment. My life had purpose and that purpose was knowing and loving God and others—starting with my husband at home. It was all the loving going on in our crooked, endearing little home in a suburb outside Los Angeles that led to me getting pregnant with our first precious gift from God.

Parenthood as Stewardship

Mama Vicki

Jan and I both cried tears of joy and gratitude when we found out that I had a little person growing inside of me. We were being granted the serious and amazing privilege of stewarding a soul for God, and that's the way we both saw it. As it sank in, it became a sobering reality. The baby was God's, but He was going to allow us a short amount of time to invest in that baby's little soul and love them as Christ would.

I asked myself, *How can I be faithful to such an important task?*

I realized that the life of my child had already begun. I was already a mommy and my responsibility for that little soul had already started. So, I tried to think about anything I could do to be a good steward. I went to my doctor's appointments faithfully, tried to make nutritional food choices, abstained from alcohol, smoke, medications, and anything that could possibly harm the baby.

I prayed fervently for our baby that they would know and love Jesus with all their heart. When I knew the baby could hear my voice, I sang hymns and songs of love to him or her and shared the simple gospel message, knowing that these were the most important words they could hear.

We took parenting classes and continued to read all the parenting books we could get our hands on. We also continued to spend time gleaning wisdom and guidance from godly couples with small children. We talked with our pastors from Grace Community Church, a large Christian church in Panorama City. The church had many pastors who ministered to the church family and we knew many of them personally. We also spoke with our parents and anyone who might be willing to impart wisdom on how to do this life-altering thing called parenting.

During this time, we met a couple of families who were homeschooling their children. We had never heard of such a thing and it was not very common at the time. In fact, these families were taking a risk, homeschooling in a societal climate not particularly supportive of children being educated at home rather than in institutional settings. We had even heard of families getting unexpected visits from The Department of Children and Family Services (DCFS) due to a report having been anonymously filed, stating that the parents were spotted with their children at a grocery store or park during school hours.

Any concerns we may have had about homeschooling were quickly put to rest by the overall maturity and well-behaved manner of the homeschool children we were meeting. We were very impressed by them. It wasn't long before we came to the conclusion that God might be calling us to homeschool our children. The thought excited and terrified me, all at the same time.

I thought to myself, *I don't know the first thing about being a mom and now I'm thinking about taking on the education of our children? What if I mess them up?*

Part II

Meet Our Five Remarkable Daughters

Ivana (23 years old)

If I were to title my life, I would call it *The Life of an Analytical Artist*. The title may perplex you, reader, but I hope it intrigues you as well. It has similarly perplexed me but what is life without a little intrigue? By entrusting my life to a good God, I have discovered that there's something wonderfully comforting about the unknown.

When I was twelve years old, I had the opportunity to live in Honduras for a couple of months. Without family or friends, and with many bilingual boundaries, I was sent into a country where children didn't have shoes, dads didn't know if they would be able to put dinner on the table at night, and moms dreamt of their babies going to school every day.

I felt like I was hit with a giant boulder when I read *Trusting God* by Jerry Bridges. I realized that, "Trust is not a passive state of mind…it is a vigorous act of the soul by which we choose to lay hold the promises of God and cling to them despite the adversity that at times seeks to overwhelm us."

I have carried this lesson with me through the greatest challenges of youth: overcoming my selfish predisposition to agonize over my future, and actively trusting that God is writing my narrative. I have learned that I simply need to hand Him the pen. Every day. Every hour.

God is writing my narrative. I have learned that I simply need to hand Him the pen.

Nothing could have better trained me to recognize and adopt this lifestyle than my years as a homeschool student in my parents' home. The path that I seem to have recently been set on—the music industry!—has propelled me to new heights of trust and hope in my relationship with the Lord. Anyone who has ever tried to make it in entertainment knows exactly what I'm talking about. Living paycheck to paycheck is a willfully precarious lifestyle—but I have discovered that my love for this nonverbal language we call music exceeds my fear of failing.

I loved homeschool. Absolutely loved it. As soon as my parents were satisfied that they had sufficiently fostered a love of learning within me, my education was put into my hands. That's right—I had the freedom to educate myself. What kid gets to do that these days? Mom would constantly check our ratio of success to not-so-successful in every subject and grade. Any time we didn't feel good about it, she changed the learning method to meet our needs.

I had the freedom to educate myself.

With the freedom to educate myself, I flew. I whizzed through kindergarten and elementary grades 1 through 6. (I let my sister Belicia catch up with me along the way. We share a deep love for gaining skills and acquiring knowledge and entertained ourselves with competitions to see who could get it faster.)

Luckily for me, I found education to be fun. It gave me a satisfying sense of pride when I would complete my grade books, excel in reading and writing and score high on tests. Feeling like a smart, capable and successful person (even as a seven-year-old) never feels like a drag. Somehow, even during the difficult subjects, Mom was able to foster that within us.

I passed the CAT exam in the 97th percentile as an eleven-year-old, and that pushed me right into high school. I took so much ownership of my school that often I would just come to Mom if I had been stuck on a problem for more than ten minutes. I was trained to research and search for an answer to my problem using all the resources I had. That is how I graduated high school at the age of fourteen with a 3.89 GPA.

My philosophy on education, developed during my homeschool years, is this: it is ultimately the child who is being educated so it is ultimately the child that should decide how they are educated!

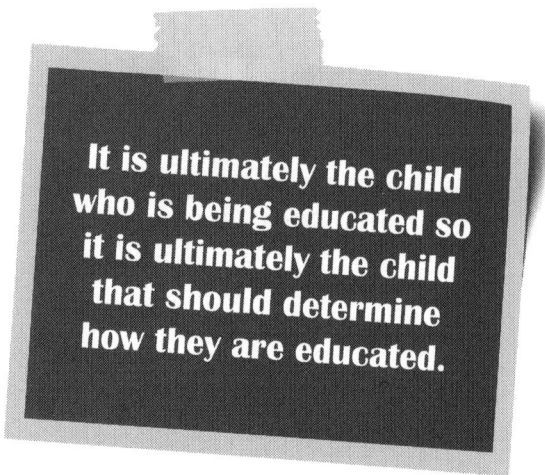

It is ultimately the child who is being educated so it is ultimately the child that should determine how they are educated.

Obviously, the key to successful homeschooling is a mother like mine. Let me explain. Mom didn't need her Masters or Ph.D. in Education to teach the five of us girls life lessons or biology lessons. That came from her. She is a dedicated scholar of people and that includes her own children. She would constantly communicate with us, as we would with her, and that kept us afloat when we were sinking under confusion or overwhelmed with our material.

Thanks to the internet, online courses and counselors who are just a phone call away, parents have endless ways to educate themselves on how to educate their kids. But the most important gift Mom gave us was herself, her time and her love.

PRODUCTIVE HOMESCHOOLING

There's nothing more a kid could ask for, even when we don't know how to ask for it, or sometimes appear to reject it.

The excuse I hear most often from new parents, particularly new moms, is that they are afraid they will fail their kids because they don't consider themselves teachers. I have two responses to that. First, by virtue of being a parent, you are teaching your children every day. You are teaching them how to think and instructing them in how to deal with problems when they face them. And secondly, homeschool is a highly effective tool that enables you to spend the necessary time ingraining in your child good values and habits, and the practical and scholarly knowledge they need to succeed in life.

Take me as an example. I have not let my fear of failure in the music industry keep me from pursuing it, and I don't let fear hold me back now. Isn't that what you want to teach your children?

During those homeschool years, I discovered my love for: grammar in literature, studying systems in government, the order of nature, and theoretical properties of music and philosophy. These are not things you would expect an "artist" to get excited about. Artists are characteristically categorized as tortured lovers that put their feelings into harmonies and write stirring lyrics. I am hardly emotional, though I feel deeply when I worship or become impassioned with anger towards evil things. Poetry was not my favorite thing in high school and I certainly did not envy the inner torment that my artist friends endured.

I am a classic tomboy. I do not care if I can't get my pedicure every week and I certainly don't mind eating saucy meatballs with my hands. During my years as a tennis player in the USTA Junior League, I could get away with that personality. Now that I actually spend every single day with tormented artists, I'm not the only one questioning myself.

You may be wondering how a highly analytical girl like me could follow her heart into the emotional whirlwind of

THE CESPEDES FAMILY

the music industry. Well, this notion was not accepted easily; it took me not one, not two, but *three* dramatic terminations in two school programs and one work opportunity to get it into my head.

I was very burdened after each of those instances of perceived failure. I felt overwhelmingly discouraged and disappointed in myself because I am the eldest of the five Cespedes girls and I felt under pressure to perform and succeed. I questioned what I was doing with my life.

It wasn't easy living up to the expectations of everybody around me. I can't blame them. Our story was known in the community and many people expected us to be big-time career women. Instead of walking around in straight skirts, pumps and blazers, I must have struck quite a picture, being this teenager wearing her dad's t-shirts over ankle-length skirts. I too would have done a double take.

Unlike my sisters, I have achieved a kind of success that is not financially secure and does not necessarily promise stability in the future. My analytical brain and planner personality could barely handle it. I have to laugh, realizing that I literally kicked and screamed my way into the music industry.

I currently work full-time finding ways to support my music dreams: session singing, studio work, accompanying, teaching, educating as a tutor for special needs students, and assistant-managing my parent's properties. My journey to recognize my musical path has been like a romantic comedy—entertaining, cheesy, emotional and downright hilarious.

Adapting to and accepting my desire to be a musician has been the greatest challenge I have experienced so far in my education and career. Whatever form my musician life takes is up to the Ruler of Heaven and Earth.

I am not worried. I am only filled with gratitude. To live the life of an analytical artist is as terrifying as it is exhilarating, so what am I going to allow to direct my attitude and emotions? As long as I trust God, fear cannot win!

Belicia (22 years old)

In 2012, I found myself enrolled in a law degree program. Here's what happened. Dad had enrolled *himself* in the program in February of that same year. He is always inclusive when it comes to our family, and confident in the academic abilities of us girls. So, he encouraged Ivana and me to enroll as well. Being a visionary, he saw the endless potential in the business world for someone with a law degree.

We thought, *Law? At fourteen and fifteen years old?*

Then we said to ourselves, *Okay, sure. We'll give it a shot.* It gave us something challenging and highly beneficial that we three could do together.

While I was enrolled in my first year of law studies, we revisited the subject of finances and business. (Spending time with my entrepreneurial dad and accompanying him to job sites had shown me that I enjoyed business and especially the financial side of things. More on that later.) My parents could see an aptitude there.

Papa Jan

When Lili (Belicia) was ten to twelve years old, she would accompany me on job walks. As we did these walks together, she listened to the job requirements of the projects we were engaging in, and absorbed the financial responsibilities of the contracts for those projects. After the meeting, I would ask her what she thought about the meeting. She often recited the scope of work and financial requirements of the contracts, verbatim.

I was often completely taken aback by her recitation of the scope of work and insights into the details of the job. It blew me away to think that our baby girl could, at such an early age, understand such complexities.

Lili is so beautiful and innocent, and yet she fully understood the intent of the words spoken by the contract managers and supervisors. We were often considering bidding on multi-million-dollar projects and it didn't faze her one bit. This girl is brilliant!

Belicia

My parents could see an aptitude there, and that's when we decided that I would be a bookkeeper. We liked the idea that bookkeeping was vocational, didn't require a degree, enabled me to work with Dad, and provided me with something to study. It was exactly what we were looking for in a career path for me. Or, so we thought, anyway.

I finished both the bookkeeping and QuickBooks courses and certifications only one month after I had enrolled in them. That's when we discovered that the bookkeeping path wasn't going to be sufficiently challenging for me but at least we were on the right track. I understood the concepts very well and enjoyed the subject matter, so we knew that I was in the right field. I just needed to shoot higher so I chose accounting.

I remember writing "Become a licensed CPA" on the top of my New Year's resolutions list on January 1st of 2014. On October 29th of that same year, I was able to put a huge checkmark beside that goal. My family is a huge party family, so it was a given that they would put together a surprise get-together for when I actually received my license.

What I didn't know was that they were already making preparations behind the scenes. For over two weeks, they had me believing that we were having a surprise birthday party for my younger sister, Briana. I was inadvertently inviting people and decorating for my own party.

PRODUCTIVE HOMESCHOOLING

On the actual day of what I believed to be Briana's surprise party, we won a volleyball tournament. I was in charge of keeping Briana out of the house and stalling until everyone arrived three hours later. That was the longest and most awkward sister date ever. Acting is not one of my gifts, so coming up with excuses to keep her away from home did not come naturally.

When I knew that everyone was in position for the surprise, and it was finally okay to bring Briana home, I blindfolded her. Then I led her into the house where everyone was waiting.

As soon as I took off her blindfold to reveal everyone waiting to celebrate her, they all became a flash mob. To my surprise, Briana jumped in and joined them.

I thought, "Well, I guess I'd better join too then!"

It took me more than a minute to realize that everyone was looking and smiling at *me*, not Briana. They grabbed me and put me in the center, while everyone proceeded to perform their solo parts and spotlight moments to the tune of *Happy* by Pharrell Williams.

I shook my head in disbelief. I couldn't imagine why everyone was there to celebrate me.

At the end of the song, they all formed a tunnel, and pushed me through it.

When I reached the end, all I could see was my dad. He was standing with a huge smile on his face, holding a large frame. Dad handed me the license.

I started smiling from ear to ear. I was almost brought to tears. It was the first time that the realization really set in.

The crowd started to chant, "Speech! Speech! Speech!"

I couldn't say a word. I was speechless. The only thing I could think to say was, "Thank you!" and "I can't believe I am now Belicia Cespedes, CPA."

THE CESPEDES FAMILY

"Thank you! I can't believe I am now Belicia Cespedes, CPA."

Whenever I tell my story or give my testimony, I refer to it as *How I Became a CPA at Seventeen*. That is how I am introduced any time I am invited to speak at national accounting conferences. Each and every time I hear that introduction, it makes my face glow pink.

I may be the youngest person in this country, and perhaps even the world, to receive my CPA license at the tender age of seventeen. (We have contacted Guinness of *The Guinness Book of World Records* and they can't confirm this, but I believe that it may be true.)

What I do know for a fact is that I have received—and accepted!—an offer from PricewaterhouseCoopers (PwC) to join their staff as a fulltime forensic accountant. I am one of their youngest employees.

PRODUCTIVE HOMESCHOOLING

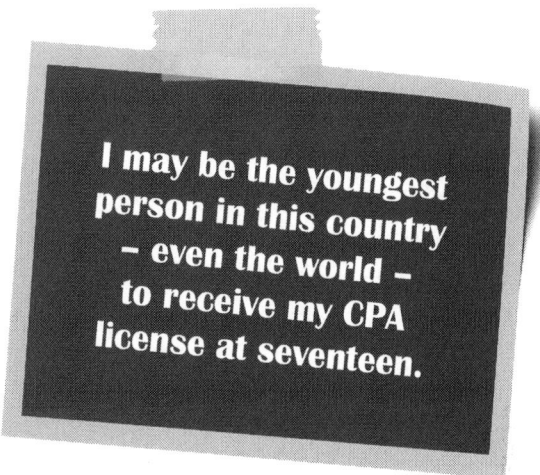

I may be the youngest person in this country – even the world – to receive my CPA license at seventeen.

So, how did a simple homeschooled girl like me achieve the CPA license at a young age, become a prolific speaker at national conventions, intern, and receive an offer for full-time employment from the nation's largest accounting firm, all while keeping myself sane? Read on.

Briana (20 years old)

My name is Briana but I go by "Bri." Upon graduating from Thomas Edison College (now Thomas Edison State University), I looked at MBA curriculum. When I saw the required 150-page essays I would have to write on the topic of supply-chain management, I was very intimidated and straight-up bored. I knew instantly that I was neither ready for that, nor convinced of the upside of pursuing this path.

That's when my dad started talking to me (as he did with each of us girls) about California Northwestern Law School. This was a program in which he had been enrolled—and excelled—before going in a different direction at the end of the first year.

THE CESPEDES FAMILY

At first, I said, "No way! I can't do law school at fifteen years old! It's impossible."

Dad wasn't easily swayed against the idea. He is and has always been the visionary of the family. He constantly pushed us girls and told us we could accomplish things outside what we thought possible. I'm so thankful to Dad for his endless encouragement and vision, especially when it comes to us girls and our potential. (I think I get a lot of my drive and stubbornness from my dad.)

As I considered law school more, I was intrigued by the case briefs. I found them to be fascinating stories involving government and a history of policy. I liked it enough to give it a shot. The only prerequisites for the school were that I have my bachelor's degree from a regionally accredited school, and take some course tests. Not long after I earned my bachelor's degree at age fifteen, I was approved to begin law coursework. I was only sixteen years old.

Just like my dad, I only studied law for one year but it proved to be an instrumental year for me. I learned that I was capable of doing a lot. I enjoyed the challenge as well as the subjects and, all in all, had a good experience.

Northwestern University required a first-year law student's exam (also known as the "baby bar") in order for a student to proceed to the second year of law school. It was a very difficult, eight-hour exam, comprised of all first-year subjects. I took this test three times (the maximum allowable) and failed it twice. This was a very difficult, eight-hour exam.

When I failed twice, I felt so hurt. To be honest, I lost motivation after the first try and I realized I didn't really want to study at this online school. I needed other suffering students around me, discussions about reasoning, and debates in class. I dreamed about attending Harvard, a brick-and-mortar law school. Perhaps one day I will.

PRODUCTIVE HOMESCHOOLING

My desire to serve in the military was growing stronger at that point and was the only pursuit on my mind. I had been talking to my parents about it for a couple years by then and doing a lot of my own research on the subject.

When I first mentioned the military, my parents were hesitant. They warmed to the idea and became more interested when I told them how I could learn a profession while serving my country. I could become a lawyer, a propulsion mechanic, even a geospatial analyst. The possibilities were wide open. I was very inspired by the idea and felt a renewed motivation to do something important.

One day, after a lot of heartfelt self-examination, I realized that I was ready to go start this chapter of my life. My parents were frightened but excited for me, and I was more than ready.

I have been accepted to the United States Air Force. Since May of 2017, I have been known as Cespedes Airman E3. As this book is being written, I have been selected as the Air Force alternate to compete for Joint Service Member of the Year.

Many people told me that, as a Christian, I was not supposed to—and shouldn't!—join the military. Moving forward with my dream in the face of such resistance has been rough. Now that I'm actually serving, people have come to accept it more and I have received more support.

I am currently a broadcast journalist in the Air Force, stationed in New Jersey. It is a seven-to-four job and then some. Writing, reading, speaking, and creating are the skills I'm currently forced to refine now.

I am right where I want to be—defending the Constitution of these great United States, joining in the U.S. Air Force's mission to protect our citizens, and being a part of that protection. I am so happy that I listened to my heart and followed my dream. I couldn't be more fulfilled.

THE CESPEDES FAMILY

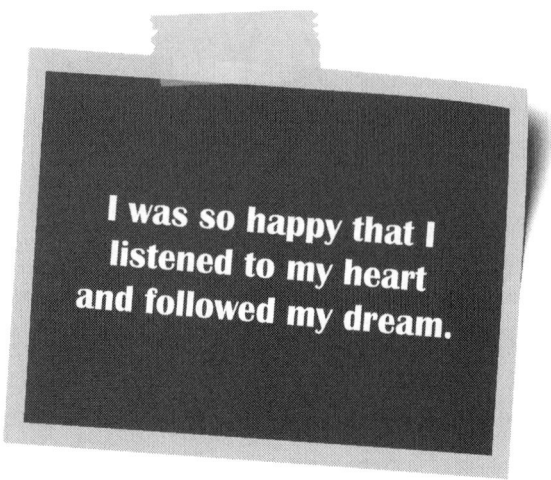

I was so happy that I listened to my heart and followed my dream.

Giana (19 years old)

My name is Giana Joy, and my name is very special to me. My parents had an agreement that Dad would name the boys and Mom would name the girls. When five girls and no boys popped out, Papa was left with no boy to name. (Sorry, Dad!)

Mom found my name on a visit to the library while she was pregnant with me. She had gone there wondering what she should name me and was searching through books of baby names. Nothing really stood out to her. Then, a book titled *Gianna* caught her eye and she picked it up. It happened to be a true story about a woman whose mother had attempted to abort her. They were already in the abortion process and somehow in the middle of it, they stopped and she was delivered alive. This baby ended up having a lot of physical disabilities and issues, but used her difficult history to find the beauty in her challenges and bring glory to God throughout her life.

PRODUCTIVE HOMESCHOOLING

Most people don't know this, but I had a twin that was miscarried around four months into the pregnancy. So, Mom named me Giana because she always believed that God had a beautiful purpose for my life. Now, here I am sharing my story with you.

I graduated from College of the Canyons (COC) with my Associates Degree in American Sign Language Interpreting at sixteen years of age. I was the youngest person to graduate at COC. I earned a 3.5 GPA overall. I also received a medal for graduating with a 3.8 GPA in the interpreting program.

To keep up my skills, I went to Georgia and spent an entire month immersing myself in deaf culture and communicating purely through my hands. I also became a counselor at camps and Bible schools for the deaf. Later that summer, I was selected to go to the interpreters' conference for the Registry for Interpreters for the Deaf (RID), the largest and most prominent organization for sign language interpreters. (All interpreters must be certified by the RID.)

As an interpreter, I signed up to never stop learning. It is a lifetime job. I will always need to improve my knowledge and skills to ensure that I am a well-rounded and efficient interpreter.

I now work for a freelance interpreting agency called Accurate Communications, and attend school at William Woods University for a regionally accredited interpreting program. I am also an ASL Interpreter Intern with the Braille Institute. Given that the school is located in Missouri, I decided to do it online so I can finish it in a year. Right now, I am gaining as much experience as I can by interpreting and utilizing my sign language, anywhere and at any time.

I am looking forward to investing in people's lives, bringing the Gospel to the deaf and growing in knowledge. I believe God expresses His will through tugging at our hearts and the movements of our hands. Will you also listen to your hands?

Eliana ("Ellie") (9 years old)

Many kids go to a building called school for a long time and they have smart, nice teachers who teach them different stuff and they get to play at recess and have lunch. They get to play with friends and have fun. Some kids are mean but most kids are kind.

School is all of life, so my school is everywhere. Learning starts when you are born and continues happening in all of life. I am learning from nature. Bugs, bees, trees and the ocean teach me about God, who made all things. It is fun to look at them and see how interesting they are—what they eat, how they grow and how they die.

PRODUCTIVE HOMESCHOOLING

School is all of life, so my school is everywhere.

I am learning all the time in all different ways. Mama says I am learning from the time I wake up to the moment I fall asleep. That's a lot of learning! I get tired just thinking about it.

When people ask me what grade I am in I say, "I'm all over the board," because I am in third, fourth and fifth grade, all at the same time. In our family homeschool, I don't have one grade. I just move on as I learn.

Mama tells me not to try to move fast because she wants me to learn well. She wants me to focus, work hard and do my best. Making mistakes is okay and actually good because you can learn from your mistakes. I don't have to be perfect but I do need to be the best I can be. And if I am not afraid of making a mistake, I will try more and learn more.

There's so much I want to learn and I'm glad I am still little so hopefully I can learn lots and lots. I want to learn as much as I can.

DISCOVERING HOMESCHOOLING

Homeschooling Found Us

Papa Jan

My love for my firstborn daughter, Ivana, was greater than anything and only increased my ardor to know truth. So, I made the big decision to put off business and begin my studies at The Master's Seminary.

Meanwhile, Vicki quit her doctoral program in psychology to raise Ivana and support me. What a partner in life and love! After five years of daily study and many sleepless nights, I earned a Master's of Divinity degree. Although Vicki did not earn a theology degree, she did as much work as I did, reading all my theology books, helping me with research and helping me write and rewrite hundreds of papers.

We learned and grew together as a couple. During those years, our family also grew to six, as we had three more girls after Ivana. We had one daughter each year of seminary!

PRODUCTIVE HOMESCHOOLING

(Ellie had not yet joined the family.) While in seminary, I met many capable, caring, skillful, godly men who were also in my program. A few became lifelong friends, including Tim Rafalovich, Michael Grisanti, and Mike Derus.

Mama Vicki

When Ivana was born, my husband and I couldn't believe how much love we had for another person and how precious she was to us. We both wanted to pour our lives and our whole selves into teaching her everything we could. It was so much fun teaching her life skills, everything from walking to tying her shoes. We even taught her some very basic sign language, like the signs for please, thank you, and more.

    Remembering what we had experienced in our own years in school, we knew that we didn't want to put our daughter in public school when she turned five. The thing we wanted most for her, above and beyond everything else in life, was a relationship with Christ. We knew that this was the most important thing and everything else paled in comparison. The school system was not set up to promote or support that priority.

    We had heard of a family who was homeschooling their children, and spent some time with them. We were instantly impressed with their children's ability to engage in conversation with us, as well as their politeness and manners, and excellent use of their time. They seemed very purposeful, enjoyed activities that were educational in nature, and appeared to have a very happy home overall.

    We started praying about homeschooling. Both Jan and I were worried that we would not do homeschooling well. We felt completely inept and very afraid of messing up our kids.

THE CESPEDES FAMILY

We felt completely inept and very afraid of messing up our kids.

When Ivana was twelve months old, I was pregnant again and close to delivering our second child. With one baby in the stroller and one in my belly, I attended the first of many Christian Home Educators Association (CHEA) annual conventions. At the convention, there were hundreds of homeschool families gathered together to support each other, share resources and curriculum, and share their experiences.

After attending the convention, I took some very simple things I had learned and began to apply them at home. One of the main concepts I had picked up was this: start homeschooling with reading, writing and arithmetic. So, I started practicing with Ivana while she was in her highchair.

I would keep crayons handy, along with a set of flash cards with both the alphabet and numbers 1 to 100. I would teach her the ABC's, teach her how to count from 1 to 10, and show her how to hold a crayon so she could scribble. We did this for five minutes at a time and, to my surprise, my little girl started learning. Those five-minute sessions expanded until they became ten-minute sessions, and then fifteen-minute sessions and so on.

PRODUCTIVE HOMESCHOOLING

By the time Ivana was two, she could hardly talk—but she could count to 100, knew the alphabet and basic phonic sounds, and was able to form written letters. I was amazed. And I thought to myself, *Surely, I have a genius on my hands. How is this possible?*

Homeschooling gave structure to our day and yet freed us from the academic prison of rigid eight-to-three schedules, lesson planning, and spending a certain number of hours per day on particular subjects.

Mama Vicki

Once our little Belicia was born in 1997, she would sit in her baby swing while I was teaching Ivana. When Ivana was two and a half years old, I would have Belicia sitting in her high chair while I asked Ivana questions. Imagine my shock when, on occasion, Belicia would answer the questions I was asking her big sister. Each time it happened, I was stunned, and yet this scenario repeated itself as each of our daughters was born.

By the time they were three years old, three of my girls could read. Even Giana, my daughter with dyslexia, was able to read simple words by the age of four. I found that each of my girls was capable of so much more at a young age than I ever would have dreamed.

I wasn't supposed to officially start homeschooling them until they were age six, but they were already reading, writing, doing math, history and science. I thought I was practicing but I was actually teaching. And, they were learning.

THE CESPEDES FAMILY

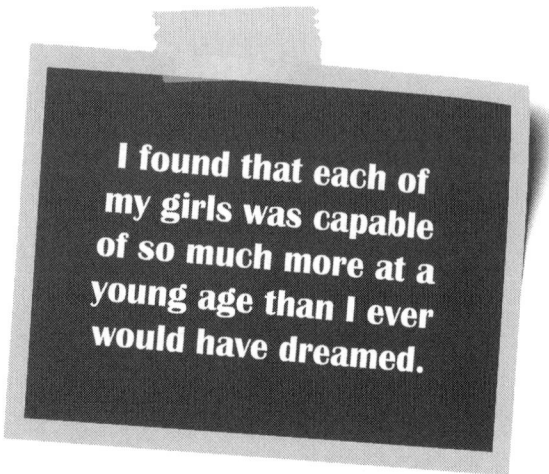

I found that each of my girls was capable of so much more at a young age than I ever would have dreamed.

Learning was fun, exciting and new. It had become a natural part of the girls' everyday lives—not an isolated activity we did on the side. It was part of them growing up and maturing. Homeschooling was life learning. It founds us and was happening naturally.

Belicia

So much of who I am, and *why* I am who I am, can be traced directly to the incredible parenting of the two wonderful people I am blessed to call my parents. As you know by now, both Mom and Dad completed kindergarten through twelfth grade at public or private schools. Then they went on to college without a clear goal of what they wanted to do with their lives, figuring that they would discover it as they went. They picked majors in subjects that sounded interesting and doable, finished their bachelor's degrees and went on to graduate studies—all without the clarity of a specific goal.

In the end, neither of my parents ended up using their degrees to earn a living. They realized that much of the

PRODUCTIVE HOMESCHOOLING

memorized knowledge they had gained was short term in nature and usually forgotten after several months of taking the class. The things they learned best, and retained longest, were the things they experienced in a hands-on way in a work environment.

Mom and Dad hoped to find a way to help us children go through the educational process in a more efficient and target-driven way. They became more vocationally minded, seeking to expose us girls as early as possible to as much as they could so we could discover our passions.

Because of some of their deeply-held convictions, Mom and Dad decided to venture into a world in which they had no experience: homeschooling. They started out at ground zero, with Mom doing some research on the topic. While they were beginning to research homeschooling, they found out they were pregnant with my elder sister, Ivana.

When Ivana was a year old and I was about ready to be born, my mother attended her first homeschool convention given by the Christian Home Educators Association. She started applying simple tips for teaching phonics, simple math, history, science, art, etc. She started doing preschool with Ivana simply as a fun and purposeful activity that lent structure to their day. I joined them as soon as I could sit in my highchair.

Little did Mom know that Ivana would start reading vigorously by the age of three, with books quickly becoming her favorite toys. Not only was Ivana reading by the age of three, she was also counting to 100, adding and subtracting, and memorizing simple things like geometric shapes, the parts of the human body and many verses of Scripture.

Mom was equally surprised when, at two years old, I started answering simple questions intended for Ivana. Apparently, I had been listening and learning, after all. Soon

THE CESPEDES FAMILY

I was able to spell my name and, by the age of three, I too was able to read.

In the meantime, Briana came along and, of course, Mom sat *her* in her highchair while she was teaching us. She wondered if the same thing would happen with Briana that had happened with Ivana and me—and sure enough, it did.

What I Learned About Learning

Mama Vicki

My girls were teaching *me* some interesting things about learning. I now see the education/learning process in the following way:

- ☞ **Step one:** The first step in the learning process is knowledge acquired by hearing, reading and watching. I think of it much like a baker going to the grocery store and acquiring all the ingredients he will need to bake a cake.
- ☞ **Step two:** The next step of true learning/education requires doing and living. Only by *integrating acquired knowledge into life* can one truly retain it. Continuing with the baker analogy, in order to bake that loaf of bread, the baker must get his hands dirty and mix together all the ingredients in a way that makes sense. Or, as John Holt once said, "Learning is not the product of teaching. Learning is the product of the activity of learners."
- ☞ **Step three:** Once you have lived the acquired knowledge, it influences and changes you, and improves your character. Now it is yours and you

are able to pass it along to someone else—to teach, to serve, to help and to comfort. Once the loaf of bread is baked, it is ready to be shared and tasted by others as part of *their* step one of learning.

Intelligence is defined as the ability to acquire *and apply* knowledge and skills. Our culture often considers someone intelligent when they are able to recite a laundry list of facts, and recall details about notable people, dates, places and events. Those things, however, are only one aspect of intelligence. It is like our baker purchasing his ingredients, memorizing the nutritional facts about them and being able to recite them verbatim—but stopping there. Or, to quote Fred Hargadon, "Because we cannot measure the things that have the most meaning, we give the most meaning to the things we can measure."

Or, as William Feather is quoted as saying: "An education isn't how much you have committed to memory, or even how much you know. It's being able to differentiate between what you do know and what you don't. It's knowing where to go to find out what you need to know, and it's knowing how to use the information once you get it."

I believe that the truly intelligent person does more than memorize bits of knowledge so that they're able to recite them back, verbatim. The truly intelligent person takes pieces of acquired knowledge and thinks about them, ponders them and meditates on them.

As they consider the pieces of knowledge they've acquired, and make connections between them and other pieces of knowledge, changes in thinking may occur and convictions may arise. In this way, knowledge becomes an agent of change, appreciation and gratitude, and a contribution to richness of character. The learning takes on a life and the learner begins to live it and do it. The intelligent person applies knowledge and gains skills out of this learning.

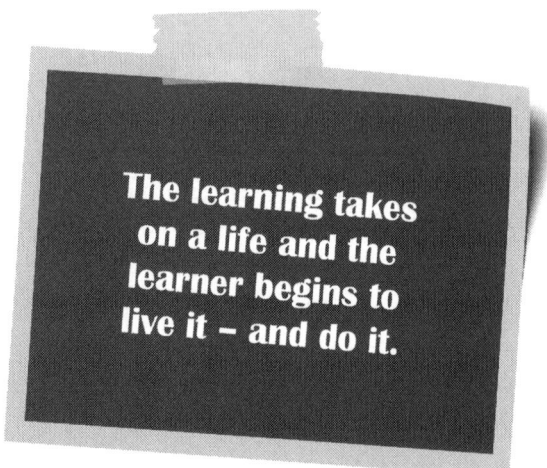

The pinnacle of learning is teaching—sharing knowledge with others so that they too may apply it first to their character, and then to the way they live their lives.

Or, to quote Aristotle, "Teaching is the highest form of understanding."

SECURING OUR FOUNDATION

Submitting Our Lives to Christ

Mama Vicki

Jan and I instinctively understood that when it came to teaching our daughters, learning would be not only taught but *caught*. Knowing that our children would learn from the way we lived our lives, we understood that we needed to model a hunger for truth and wise living, even as we acknowledged that it would be done imperfectly. Thankfully, I have discovered that children have no problem being gracious with the imperfection of their parents. What exasperates them is hypocritical parents who demand something from their children that they don't demonstrate in their own lives.

We realized that acting on the privilege of homeschooling our girls required a solid foundation. We knew that, now that Christ was our Savior, He also needed to be our Lord and we needed to submit all areas of our lives to Him.

THE CESPEDES FAMILY

That meant that, as the parents and teachers of our girls, we needed to examine our lives, be willing to humble ourselves and turn away from sin and anything displeasing to God, and be earnest in our efforts to improve in areas where we were weak. And finally, we had to remain in a constant mode of learning and putting that learning into action, especially if we were going to teach that to our children.

I have many memories of acknowledging my weakness and asking forgiveness from my husband and daughters. They were gracious with me then, and they are gracious with me today, as some of my weaknesses are still with me. (Just take a peek into my office and you will see what looks like the aftermath of a hurricane.)

Although I have struggled much in the past, today I am comfortable in my perpetual state of imperfection. I now realize how it highlights the beauty of mercy and forgiveness all the more in my life and causes me to live in a perpetual state of thankfulness.

OUR HOMESCHOOLING ADVENTURE BEGINS

Redefining Education for Ourselves

Mama Vicki

When Jan and I first discovered homeschooling and started giving it consideration as a serious option for our family, I found myself asking, *What is education anyway?*

According to Webster's Dictionary, "Education is the process of receiving or giving systematic instruction; a body of knowledge acquired while being educated; information about or training in a particular field; an enlightening experience."

Wikipedia defines it this way: "Education is the process of facilitating learning, or the acquisition of knowledge, skills, values, beliefs, and habits. Educational methods include storytelling, discussion, teaching, training, and directed research. Education frequently takes place under the guidance of educators but learners may also educate themselves. Education can take place in formal or informal settings and any experience that has a formative effect on the way one thinks, feels, or acts may be considered educational."

This is the definition that hit me: "...Learners may also educate themselves. Education can take place in formal or informal settings and *any* experience that has a formative effect on the way one thinks, feels, or acts may be considered educational." [Emphasis added.]

I could totally relate to that definition because it was exactly what I was experiencing since becoming a Christian. I was hungry to learn, and wanted to take in information and then apply it to my life. I wanted to a learn how to live in a way that honored Christ and I was doing all I could to do just that.

It was happening—not in a school setting but in all areas of my life. It was happening in my home, with my husband, in the homes of others, in the grocery store, in my car as I listened to sermons or audio books, and in my bed as I cried out for wisdom and was granted it. In every setting of life, I was being educated and I was learning. This was the way I wanted to educate my children, using life as the schoolroom.

Setting Goals to Match Our Values

Mama Vicki

Believe it or not, academic success and accelerated study were not the goals of our homeschooling. Jan and I wanted our girls to be truly educated and specifically Christian educated. The foundation of all that has transpired is God. He is the mover and shaker. He is the reason and the motivation, and He gets all the glory.

We wanted our girls to know and love Christ so much that they felt compelled to feast on His Word and His wisdom and passionate about honoring Him with every desire, thought, decision and moment of their time.

We wanted our girls to be hungry for truth and eager to apply it to their lives, and we wanted them to learn skills that they could use in the service of others. We wanted them to love the process of learning and to recognize that knowledge was never meant to be kept for oneself alone but shared with others, as others had shared with them. Teaching our girls to sit still and not grumble about it was the first step.

We would have been satisfied if these goals had been reached apart from degrees or licenses earned and age ceilings broken. To us, true success in our girls' education has been evidenced by the fact that their hearts bear godly fruit, especially now as adult women who are walking with the Lord and who are kind and serve others. Their godly character is the greatest jewel in our crown and the only one that really matters.

Values-Centered Education

Mama Vicki

Jan and I wanted the privilege of being able to instill in our daughters' little hearts and minds the values that were most important to us. I do believe that one of the most important things we did was teach our girls about God, and keep His Word as our primary textbook in our home. Character training was essential to our success in homeschooling and it led to very practical outcomes.

So, what outcomes were we looking for and how did we expect to reach them?

THE CESPEDES FAMILY

Our prayers were that our homeschooling would lead to children who would be:

- Faith-centered (Christ-gospel centered);
- Centered in love of learning;
- Centered in love of service (using learning and skills to serve others);
- Able to self-initiate and learn independently, even when it was challenging;
- Focused on making the most of their time;
- In possession of the proper perspective on the value and precious nature of time and an understanding that it should not be wasted;
- Aware that focused time needed to be balanced with childhood play and wonder;
- Proficiency-centered and in possession of knowledge without being bogged down by the need to memorize voluminous facts for the short term;
- Centered on their unique gifts and interests;
- Practical-skills oriented (practical-skill development that could be used to serve and help others, as well as to provide an income when and if needed);
- Budget conscious, with the goal that each daughter would finish their formal institutional education with no debt to burden them in the future;
- Long-term expertise focused (if you find what you love to do early, then you can get practical experience sooner);
- Tailoring their education toward depth of learning in their area of expertise and taking the time to go deep and wide in that field before life gets full with other wonderful things; and

☞ Apprenticeship focused (finding what they love, then finding those who are best at those things and seeking mentorship from them).

Homeschooling as Discipleship

Mama Vicki

The only way we found to reach these outcomes was to realize that homeschooling was another name for discipleship. Discipleship was our method, the Word of God our primary textbook, and the focus on loving God and others our daily creed and focus. Well, that's what we strived for, anyway. It was the general pattern of our lives but we failed often.

It is truly baffling to me when I think about what God did in respect to the girls' academics. It turned out that the academic aspect of their homeschooling was quite supplemental in nature. Yes, we did comply with California State Department of Education requirements, but to the minimum level required. Most of our time was spent in purposeful and contented Christian discipleship.

Many people ask me, "How do you account for the girls' amazing acceleration and academic achievements? How did this happen?"

Of course, I tell them the truth: "God did it! I wouldn't have even known how to plan for it or execute it."

Most people aren't entirely satisfied with that answer so I try to paint a picture of how we did it.

THE CESPEDES FAMILY

Character Training

Papa Jan

What I learned in seminary became the solid foundation for my budding faith. I also instinctively understood that it would be a solid foundation for our girls' education and future lives. The doctrine and the attitude toward Scripture taught in seminary profoundly impacted the way I raised my family. Our girls grew up memorizing and reciting the Scriptures I studied.

One of their favorite activities was marching around the room, stomping, and reciting Proverbs 15:15: "All the days (stomp!) of the afflicted are evil (stomp!), but he who has a merry heart (stomp!) has a continual feast (loud palatial clicks like we were riding horses)."

It brings a smile to my face every time I remember that. And now that Eliana (whom we call little Ellie) can read and write well beyond her eight years, she too can recite those same passages with just as much glee and enthusiasm as her sisters before her.

The wisdom of the Proverbs was easily understood by our girls, so we taught them that, "…a gentle answer turns away wrath." (Proverbs 15:1).

I am happy to say that the girls have clearly internalized this wisdom and operate by this life code (even if they are too humble to recognize that wisdom in themselves). Consider the wisdom in this passage of Scripture at Proverbs 10:13—23:

> [13] On the lips of the discerning, wisdom is found,
> But a rod is for the back of him who lacks [a]understanding.

¹⁴ Wise men store up knowledge,
But with the mouth of the foolish, ruin is at hand.
¹⁵ The rich man's wealth is his ᵃfortress,
The ruin of the poor is their poverty.
¹⁶ The ᵇwages of the righteous is life,
The income of the wicked, punishment.
¹⁷ He is *on* the path of life who heeds instruction,
But he who ignores reproof goes astray.
¹⁸ He who conceals hatred *has* lying lips,
And he who spreads slander is a fool.
¹⁹ When there are many words, transgression is unavoidable,
But he who restrains his lips is wise.
²⁰ The tongue of the righteous is *as* choice silver,
The heart of the wicked is *worth* little.
²¹ The lips of the righteous feed many,
But fools die for lack of ᶜunderstanding.
²² It is the blessing of the Lord that makes rich,
And He adds no sorrow to it.
²³ Doing wickedness is like sport to a fool,
And *so is* wisdom to a man of understanding.

This is the mindset that we wanted our girls to understand, embrace and nurture within themselves. We knew that it would not merely save them from error, but reveal to them the beauty of living life wisely, according to Scripture.

THE CESPEDES FAMILY

Ivana

My earliest memories of homeschooling involved waking up early, around 6:00 in the morning, and rushing downstairs. On some days as we got a little older, we woke up before Mom and Dad and would go in and wake them up. That's how excited we were to start our day. We knew that the earlier we started our day, the earlier we would get to play.

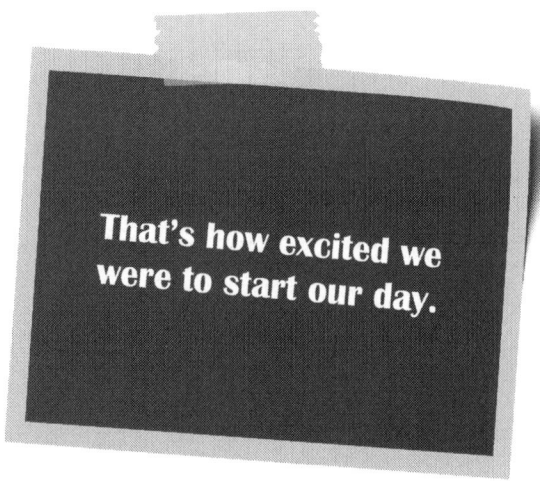

Before breakfast, we had devotional time. That was an hour we spent in Bible time, usually led by Mom. Then Dad would come in and teach us Proverbs, going through each one and teaching us to recite them. There was a series of books called *Proverbs for Parenting* which broke things down in such a way that was simple for kids to understand. We came up with routines, all sorts of things to help us remember the Proverbs.

The most memorable one was Proverbs 15:15. We created a marching routine to that one. Dad would have us march around the breakfast table reciting the Proverb and matching our steps to its rhythm. We added our own little sounds and noises as we marched. We had a whole routine going.

We created routines for a lot of the Proverbs. By the time we finished, it was usually around 8:00 in the morning. That's when we were really young, anyway. As we got a little older, we slept in a little bit later.

After we had breakfast and helped Mom clean up, we jumped right into school. There were no distractions—no morning cartoons or TV shows. We went right from getting time in the Word into breakfast and then character training from Mom. The types of character training would vary from morning to morning. Sometimes she taught us character training through books.

Mom wanted to train us proactively, not reactively, to teach us how to handle a situation rightly before it happened. She always tried to help equip us, to make it easier to do what was right. Sometimes she used little things she had prepared to teach us character lessons. These included proactive training, where we role-played situations and acted out what we would do, should do, and shouldn't do if those situations arose in real life. It was a time of lots of giggles but the lessons stuck.

My mother was and is a very studious woman of God. She always got up around four o'clock in the morning, went right into her prayer closet and shut the door. She always spent that time in the morning with God, talking to Jesus about whatever was on her heart at the time. Then, around the breakfast table, she would say to us, "Girls, this is what the Lord brought to my attention this morning. Here's what I'm meditating on…"

I felt that this was very much a ministry from Mom to us. She would even say to us, "I want to minister this to you girls so you can be encouraged by it and taught by it. I want your character and your lives to be informed by wisdom and truth." She knew that if our lives were informed by truth, we would live Christ-centered and Christ-honoring lives and we would be thinking rightly.

Belicia

I grew up in a very tight and loving family where God was the center. We had our daily routine and we knew what to expect, day in and day out. We would wake up early in the morning, have family devotions around the breakfast table, and get to school (which was at home, of course). School time was a time we looked forward to. We would all get together to sing songs, recite Scripture and read a Bible story. We would say the Pledge of Allegiance, and recite our numbers, time tables, states of the U.S., parts of the body—you name it!

Our school education was always more than just training in academics, but also training in character. Our parents wanted to instill in us from the beginning both a Biblical mindset and the proper priority of a relationship with God.

Briana

During our elementary school years, we would normally wake up at 6:00 in the morning. All four of us girls would scamper downstairs for devotional time and breakfast. (We were little eating-machines!) We would always have Bible time first and *then* eat. That was the rule of the household: "No Bible, no breakfast."

My parents focused on our hearts first thing in the morning so that we would have right attitudes and begin the day grateful that we were alive, healthy and able to have fun. Every morning we had the Gospel spelled out for us. Then Mom would start the lessons.

Life was simple and fun—filled with family and family friends, church activities, tennis lessons and tournaments, play dates, and of course, food.

Ellie

In our homeschool, Mommy teaches me about God and the Bible. We read the Bible every morning, we memorize verses, and we talk about Jesus and the Gospel. Mommy teaches me more about obedience and kindness than she does about math and English because it doesn't matter how smart you are—it matters how kind you are. Mama says there are only two things I need to remember to do every day: love God and love others.

So, when I wake up, I go straight to Mama. After snuggle time and Mama prison time (a game we play where Mama hugs me and doesn't let me go until I squirm out), I bring Mama my kids' Bible. (I have a pink one now for bigger girls. My favorite color is hot pink so I think my Bible is really pretty.)

We pray to God and read the Bible. Mama tells me, "Look for Jesus in every story!" I try to find Him but sometimes it is hard. At those times, Mama helps me and then I understand more. One day I will be able to study the Bible all by myself but right now Mama is my study buddy.

Socialization Without Age Limitations

Mama Vicki

People are often concerned about how socialization occurs in the homeschool home since the students are not in the larger school system, mixing and relating with their peers.

In our home, the socialization process was not segregated by age. Our girls learned to mix socially with people of

THE CESPEDES FAMILY

various ages, and in various seasons of life, occupations, and even residencies in countries around the globe. Our open-door hospitality policy brought into our lives people from all over the world, as well as people from our community. Children that were the same ages as the girls came over but also people ranging from newborns to ninety-year-olds.

So, our daughters had a rich and mature socialization that can still be seen today in how comfortable they are relating to little ones, to peers, to seniors, to professionals, to the poor, and to the rich. They are able to socialize with anyone and everyone and know how to carry themselves and behave in a way that is acceptable to society.

HOMESCHOOLING REGULATIONS

Operating as a Home-Based Private School

We decided to operate our homeschool program as a home-based private school. Each October we filed our private-school affidavit with the State of California, maintained required school records and provided instruction in the required courses.

I still remember the day I filed my first affidavit. I was so nervous, afraid I was going to do it incorrectly. It was nerve-wracking but it was also exciting. I had Ivana and Belicia do it with me, and they helped me choose the name of the school. We chose Magnum Opus Preparatory, named after a line from *Charlotte's Web* that referred to Charlotte's greatest work, her magnum opus—having her baby spiders. I felt that Jan and I raising our four girls at the time to be godly young women was *our* greatest work. It was our magnum opus, so the name was a perfect fit.

Prior to this, I had attended numerous homeschool conferences in preparation for this great task. It was so thrilling to see families from all over the nation seeking to honor God in the same way and seeking to teach their children a love for learning.

Some families filed affidavits. Other families were part of charter schools. Still others did ISPs (Independent Study Programs). Each family has to decide what works best for them.

In our case, Jan knew me well enough to realize that if we had been under the umbrella of an ISP, I would have been overly burdened by all the assignments, deadlines, and classes outside the home. The frenzy and pressure of this would have distracted me from our primary desire and goal of discipleship. I needed simple and slow to maintain a heart of rest, clarity, and peace in the process.

As such, the private affidavit was a huge blessing for us. It afforded me complete freedom to prioritize discipleship while still getting to the courses required by state regulation. I thrive on flexibility because it leaves me free to look for and seize spontaneous opportunities. This approach seemed to serve all of us well.

Still, there were days when I questioned myself, even felt guilty that my inability to be a "supermom" would keep my girls from benefitting from the opportunities offered through other channels of education, including ISPs, charter schools, public schools, institutional private schools, etc. I had to work really hard to keep from comparing what looked like our simplistic, thrift-store version of home education to all the fancy bells and whistles that other kids were enjoying.

Again and again, I had to remind myself that I could never, and would never be able to, give my girls all—but if I gave them Jesus, that would be more than enough. God is big enough and powerful enough to fill in the gaps in their lives and education that they need filled. And He will be faithful to do just that. My sweet fellow mommies, let us rest in those truths, so we can lay down those stressful heart obstacles that would steal our peace, our joy and more importantly, our focus from the most important things.

A big thank you to my husband for his leadership and guidance in this area. I cannot express enough how grateful I am to him for allowing me this tremendous privilege of homeschooling our girls. He worked long and hard to provide for us so I could be free to do this. It is one of the greatest gifts that he has given me, besides helping me come to know Christ. He is a man precious beyond description.

The Finances of Operating as a Private School

When you choose to be part of a charter program, you receive a monetary allowance because the state is receiving funds for your child's enrollment. We chose to be a private school instead, so we forfeited those funds. Many of our close friends knew how tight our finances were for most of our homeschooling years. And we were often asked how we were able to afford this kind of home-based educating without those funds.

I recall several years of living with a monthly grocery budget of eighty dollars to feed six people. There were a few years when finances were so tight, kind, anonymous friends left us a basket containing the makings of our Thanksgiving supper. Meanwhile our friends, the Derus family (Mike and Tammy), gave us money so we could buy Christmas gifts for our girls.

THE CESPEDES FAMILY

We had to work really hard and be frugal in order to remain a homeschool family paying out of pocket for all of our daughters' educational supplies and activities. I became a faithful coupon clipper and tried to help Jan in all his efforts to bring in income. Even during seasons that were very tight for us financially, my wonderful husband never wavered in his commitment to keep me home with the girls and we never went without enough to share.

The following are some of the methods we used to make ends meet:

- We purchased most of our school supplies from garage sales. You would commonly find us in our car on Saturday mornings, praying for God to provide the needed supplies, clothes, and household items for our family at local garage sales. It is truly incredible how often He provided exactly what we needed, if not more. Garage sales and now thrift stores are great resources for keeping costs down;
- We got to know families that had kids ahead of ours in homeschool and bought their used books and resources;
- I frequented used homeschool curriculum sales held year-round throughout the country, especially when I needed a specific curriculum that was popular and expensive;
- I created a co-op with a few other homeschool mommies and we each taught a subject to our kids, at no cost to any of us;
- I used one textbook and made copies of worksheets for my girls;
- The correspondence high school we used was very inexpensive and the cost included all administrative requirements, as well as textbooks;

PRODUCTIVE HOMESCHOOLING

☞ Some of the girls attended our community college during their junior and senior years of high school, so tuition was waived. (Some community colleges waive tuition for dual enrollment for juniors and seniors in high school who are taking courses to satisfy both high school and college requirements simultaneously);

☞ When our girls were ready to attend College of the Canyons full time, things were extremely tight financially, so much so that they qualified for the Pell Grant and Governor's tuition-waiver program. The girls were able to save enough money from the Pell Grant to take care of all their books and supplies, as well as all the CLEP exams, ACE accredited courses, and units required for their bachelor's degrees at Thomas Edison State University. Ivana and Belicia were able to use some of the leftover funds to help pay for their graduate degrees as well;

☞ The bachelor's degrees were significantly less expensive because we used a non-conventional, regionally accredited college. This college allowed the girls to:

* use up to ninety units of community college credits (free to them due to the Pell grant and tuition waiver);
* use CLEP exams, which cost eighty dollars for three-to-twelve college-credit units, depending on the exam. Most were three credits but some were six-unit credits, with languages being worth up to twelve; and
* use any other ACE accredited courses which the girls did online for an average of about one hundred dollars per three college units.

THE CESPEDES FAMILY

In the end the Pell Grant paid entirely for their bachelor's degrees, even though the degrees were earned in a way that was outside the conventional box.

- ☞ For extended educational trips and adventures, like our American History Train Adventure, we took the Amtrak train cross country, stayed at super inexpensive lodging or our friends' homes, and ate inexpensive food purchased from grocery stores;
- ☞ We always traveled after Labor Day for the lowest prices on lodging or transportation fares; and
- ☞ We were extremely frugal at home, which helped us to save for those adventures and memory-making treats, like the girls' annual trip to Yosemite with Papa.

State Requirements

At the time of this writing, there is no law in California that prohibits homeschooling, but there is no specific law allowing it either. You might ask, "So, how can we legally homeschool our children?"

I recommend a visit to the Home School Legal Defense Association website (www.hslda.org). There you will find a tremendous amount of important and helpful information related to homeschooling. I suggest that you read and consider it carefully before deciding whether or not homeschooling is right for your family.

HOMESCHOOLING CURRICULUM AND ROUTINE

Redeeming Our Time

Mama Vicki

As Jan and I lived out our pursuit of God and His truth, we were always aware of the great responsibility we carried in our role as parents and stewards of the lives of those most precious to us—our daughters. The enormity of that responsibility and privilege was sobering and scary, to say the least.

We realized that time is like a vapor, and passes away quickly. I felt a real urgency to be a good steward of the minutes, hours, days, months and years that our children would be entrusted to our care. I earnestly wanted to be productive and redeem the time given to whatever extent I could, no matter how long or short that time turned out to be.

THE CESPEDES FAMILY

My commitment to redeeming our time affected the way I thought about each day. It influenced everything from the way I decided what to teach and not to teach, to the activities in which we participated, the skills we sought to develop, and more.

Your own personal perspective related to the things you consider productive, your goals, your time, and your priorities should be on your mind constantly and informing your homeschooling decisions daily. Lesson planning is great, but for me, I felt it was imperative to leave large cushions of open time. These were used for everything from spontaneous teaching opportunities that arose from time to time, to following the unexpected learning trail of one of our kids, or attending to the unique needs of others. I was grateful that I had left those cushions so that we could have the joy and privilege of meeting those opportunities and needs at the drop of a hat.

Ellie

When I was still a baby and just learning to walk, I liked Mama to read me books. I would get a book and give it to Mama and she would read it to me. Some of my favorite books were *Love You Forever, Are You My Mother?, Cat In the Hat*, and my baby Bible. I think that all the books Mama read to me led me to starting to read when I was only three.

Mama told me that when I was a tiny baby in my crib, I had a basket and in it was my baby Bible and some toys. In the morning, she would come in and find me sitting in my crib, flipping through the pages of my Bible.

For school time, we did charts. Mama had lots of charts with pictures, and on the charts were lots of things to learn. We started with ABC's, moved on to numbers, and learned to count to one hundred. I learned about colors, shapes, days of the week, the body, the Ten Commandments, the Pledge of Allegiance, books of the Bible, Scripture verses, and the planets. (That's all I can remember at the moment.)

I was only two when Mama started using hand motions to teach me the Gospel. It went like this: "Jesus is God, who came dooowwwwn from Heaven. He became a baby, just like you. (Tickle Ellie.) He suffered and died on the cross for our sins, but He didn't stay dead, No! On the third day, He rose again, and He's alive! Jesus is alive! And He went up, up, up, up, up… (Go up on tippy toes and reach for the sky) to Heaven. He's going to come back one day to judge the living and the dead, and His kingdom will go on forever and ever and ever and ever and ever and ever. Amen!"

When I was about two, I liked to dance to the song, *Me Without You* by TobyMac. I would always jump on the jumpy part, kick my legs and do all kinds of moves. I danced for a long time and made my family smile. When I was two, it was also my job to feed the dogs. As I poured the dog food, I would always miss the bowl but the dogs didn't mind.

After feeding the dogs, Mama and I would go to the garage and get carrots to give to our horse, Samson. I was scared of him at first. When I got used to him, I asked Mama if I could go down and see him by myself, but she said no.

As I said, I was reading by age three. On my fourth birthday, Mama told me to throw away all of my pacifiers. I wanted to keep them so badly.

"Do you want to be a big girl?" Mama asked me.

I nodded yes.

"Then throw away all of your pacifiers."

So, I did. But when I was six, I found an old pacie and slept with it. I still have it somewhere but I don't know where I put it.

THE CESPEDES FAMILY

Belicia

My mom realized that she did not have geniuses on her hands, after all. The truth was that our young minds were capable of so much more than she thought possible. Once she realized that, she decided to open her mind, think outside the box and not set limits on what was possible for us girls.

Mom was determined to start us on a primary-school program even though we were not yet six years old. Even though they were not legally mandated to school us until we reached age six, my parents decided to abide by state regulations. Mom put together a kindergarten curriculum based on a local school district, and we were able to do it. It took some time and patience, but Mom could see the little light bulbs going off in our heads.

Our parents decided to allow us to go at our own pace. They would let us accelerate in those areas where we were strong and slow us down in the areas where we were weak. They also prioritized foundational skill building in the three R's—reading, writing and arithmetic. It wasn't until Ivana was six that my parents declared themselves to be their own private school by way of the registration of a Private Affidavit through the California Department of Education.

As I mentioned earlier, we woke up in the mornings around 7:00 and had our daily routine that we knew by heart and expected day in and day out. In addition to the activities I mentioned earlier, we played games as we learned addition, subtraction and multiplication, and had flashcard competitions to see who could answer the fastest. Papa gave us geography tests to see who could fill out the U.S.A. map or the world map the quickest. It was so much fun.

We would take a break to run around and play outside before coming back in for a snack. Then it was time for quiet study hall. Each of us picked up our own books, and spent concentrated time working hard and focusing. We would raise our hand if we had a question and Mom would help. This usually went on for about two hours. Then it was time for lunch, followed by an entire hour to play outside, unless we wanted to help Mom prepare food for suppertime.

Around one o'clock in the afternoon, we had our two-hour quiet time in our room. This was a naptime for the younger ones (or any of us who wanted a nap). For those who weren't sleepy, this was a time for reading, journaling, listen to audio books, or quietly playing. I have to admit, until we were nine or ten years old, most of us slept during this quiet period.

The afternoons were set aside for service. This might include anything from doing housework at home, visiting seniors, making meals for sick people or babysitting other children. To Mom, this was the most important part of the day.

Learning and Play

Mama Vicki

At every step along the way, I reminded myself that I wanted my girls to *love* learning. So, I tried as best I could to connect subjects with real life in ways that young children would most enjoy. I am not by nature a very creative or adventurous person, but I tried to imagine the types of things that might improve the likelihood of enjoyment. Sometimes, that was something as simple as moving the lesson outdoors. Or, sometimes it meant role playing, or interviewing someone else, such as an expert in a certain subject, someone with a particular role, or an excellent or winsome character. Sometimes I even added food to the lesson. (That last one seemed to work especially well.)

I asked myself, *If I were a child, how would I best like to learn this? And how can I use that knowledge/lesson in real life?*

I recommend doing all we can as homeschool moms to seek to make it as easy, as enjoyable and as practically useful to our kids as possible. If you were a child, wouldn't you want it that way?

I wanted to transition my girls to independent learning as soon as I thought them capable. I knew that by allowing their education to become their own as soon as possible, I would be giving them wings to fly, opening up limitless possibilities for them and preparing them for independent life learning.

Over time, I could see the girls developing intellectual curiosity and a love for learning. I could see that they were ready to initiate learning and education on their own. Best of all, I eventually saw convictions growing, and watched them delight in taking on the responsibility of continuing the life-long process of learning.

Briana

Let me reach back into my memory and describe for you the wonderful home in which I was raised and prepared for life. My daily life as a youngling was comprised of having half the day for school and the other half for play. It was the best thing ever. I loved my time spent outside playing with my sisters or with my "stick eater" hedge shears, as I called them. Many an hour was dedicated to digging up mounds of dirt or imagining some grand epic with my hot wheels.

I realize now that, throughout my schooling, I could have spent even more time letting myself be a child. I could have spent hours enjoying being entertained by my shovels and sticks instead of always dreaming of the future. This doesn't mean that I didn't literally spend hours digging holes and building forts, but I now realized I could have spent more time just enjoying being a kid.

I was always filled with imagination in both playtime and school, and I was especially fascinated by history. The events that take place in our world seem so unreal sometimes, and it was so exciting for me to learn from lessons from the crazy heroes and villains from the past.

Even during my time as a law student, many of the cases I read featured stories of deranged people whose absurd actions led to the creation of the laws that govern us today. There were times in my life when I wondered whether my homeschool upbringing was a good match for me—but I have to admit that my fascination with world history was fostered in me as I grew up in the Cespedes home.

Honestly, I did get to be a kid in so many ways that many kids never experience. For example, I was taught about nature and allowed to develop a fascination for it. I was taught to be in awe of even the smallest critters slithering around in our backyard (which was always a grove of trees with plenty of dirt for making mud pies.) I could study in a tree or alongside my dogs.

At the same time that I was given room to be a kid, I was also taught to strive for excellence. Being in our house was always intentional. The things we did had purpose and we were intentional about what, why, and how we did whatever it was we were doing at any given time. My sisters and I were exposed to environments, circumstances and people that facilitated our maturing process. We were, for example, constantly surrounded by the church and older folks. That gave me a taste for mature interaction far earlier than most of my peers.

I had to identify my goals in life sooner than other children and was held to a higher standard. I appreciated the challenge.

THE CESPEDES FAMILY

Briana

I hope I've been able to paint a raw, realistic picture of what homeschooling was like for me—both the struggles and advantages it brought me.

I look forward to homeschooling my own kids because I am convinced that a child can develop greater abilities and experience longer-lasting character pruning with their parents guiding their education. By homeschooling, I will be the one choosing curriculum that challenges my children to think outside the system of education, rather than the curriculum being dictated by the government.

Education is a lifestyle rather than a box to simply check off on life's to-do list. I want my children to learn *how* to truly learn, and I want them to *love* to learn. The most intelligent individuals are the ones who know how to learn. I am very grateful for my education because it provided greater opportunities for me to obtain the skills and resilience needed for true learning.

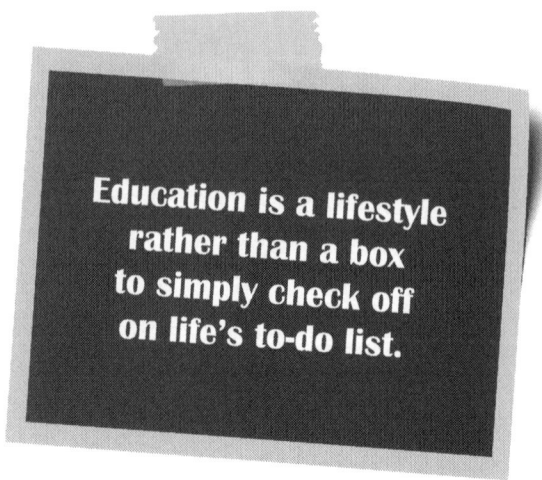

PRODUCTIVE HOMESCHOOLING

Now that I know how to learn, I can acquire much more knowledge. I want the same for my kids. Sometimes a kid will not even realize how much they enjoy learning until they are mature enough to think about more than their next meal and the next bug they might play with in the dirt. If a child can learn how to learn then their focus will narrow when they mature, and it will be easier for them to identify their truest passion—or something that brings many or most of their passions together.

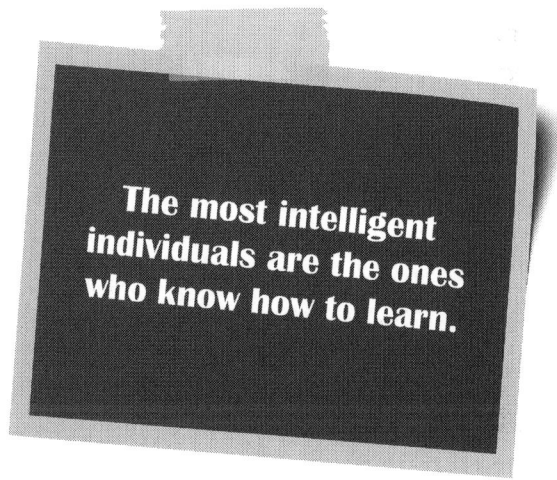

The most intelligent individuals are the ones who know how to learn.

Homeschooling with Field Trips

Ivana

We had a field trip every few days to a week. We went on a field trip any time we finished a grade. It could be as simple as a visit to the local ice cream parlor or a trip to Knotts Berry Farm. Mom also took us on a couple of field trips to the East Coast. We traveled by Amtrak train the entire way there. Those train trips left me with such vivid memories, I will never forget them.

One time we were traveling to the East Coast, and on the very first day of the trip, Belicia and I witnessed a drug dealer being arrested on the train. The next day, the two of us were playing cards in the lounge car when an autistic gentleman entered the car, loudly and violently sobbing. His cries went on for about ten minutes. Neither my sister nor I knew what to do. We were only nine and ten years old, respectively.

Some wonderful Southern Baptist women were on the train and came into the lounge car to try to help. They started laying hands on the man and calling on the Holy Spirit to help heal him. "Jesus," they prayed aloud, "we pray that you bless him…" Seeing these women praying over this heartbroken autistic man was so fantastic and such a colorful experience.

The conductor ended up having to stop the train. He came into the car, along with security. They escorted the man off the train and had him transported to the hospital. Apparently, the man had been threatening suicide for reasons unbeknownst to everyone on the train. He was yelling, "Somebody kill me! Or, I'm going to jump off this train!"

On the third night of the trip, we fell asleep in our economy-class train seats. Very early in the morning, I was awakened by the sound of a lady in front of me yelling at one of the female attendants on the train.

"Ma'am," the attendant was explaining to the passenger, "we are doing everything we can! We have just gotten word that a train derailed in front of us…and it was a mile-long freight train. For the past two days, they've been removing one box car at a time with a large crane."

Thanks to a six-hour delay caused by the train derailment, we were late getting into New York and missed the first half of our Broadway show, *Wicked*. Along the way, we had visited various other East Coast locales as well, including Boston, Philly, D.C. and Virginia.

You might be surprised when I tell you that this trip to the East Coast was the best trip *ever*. I was traveling with a suitcase filled with books. I had made it a goal to read twelve books on that trip, all of them biographies. We had great experiences and saw many friends and, all in all, it was totally awesome. We treasured the very same things that would have upset others because we recognized what great life experiences they were, and how lucky we were to be having them. That was a quintessential Cespedes family trip—filled with sweet moments and funny memories that make for great stories later.

Here's another great example of an experience that many people would have found terribly upsetting—many people, but not a Cespedes girl. I was on a date at Denny's, eating a plate of nachos. In the middle of enjoying my nachos, I nearly bit into a bolt the size of a thumb.

I threw my hands up in the air and said, "Yes! Free food!"

I knew that, in order to make up for what had happened, Denny's was about to bring me whatever I wanted off the menu. That absurd perspective on life is shared by all of us Cespedes girls. We are all very comfortable with change and less-than-ideal situations. I know this roll-with-it attitude and outlook on life has served me well.

Briana

As an avid history buff, one of the memories I cherish most is a field trip we took to the East Coast. I loved getting to experience history at the actual historical sites, like standing where the militia fought, and walking the same cobblestone streets that the founders walked. It made the past come to life and become real.

THE CESPEDES FAMILY

The Accelerated Track

Mama Vicki

I believe that one of the things that made ours such a productive homeschooling adventure was starting very young with our girls. We taught them to obey right away, all the way, and in a happy way. This led the way to learning how to wait patiently, focus intently and work diligently, all of which later brought the fruit that most people are interested in—namely accelerated academic success. Below, the girls give you their perspective of homeschooling on the accelerated track.

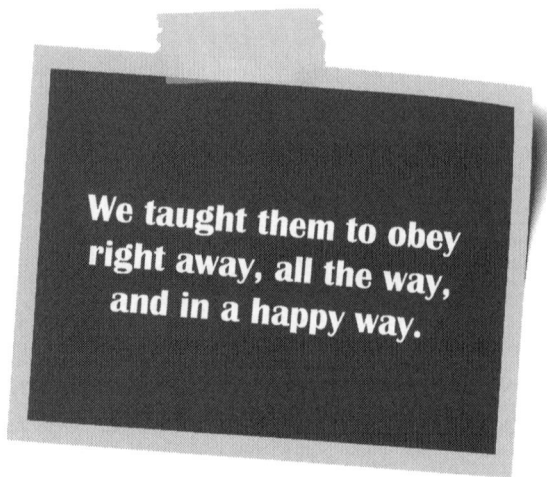

Belicia

By the time we graduated middle school and were going into high school, Ivana and I were only eleven and ten years old, respectively.

PRODUCTIVE HOMESCHOOLING

Now you may ask, "How could you have known for sure that you girls were ready for high school at ten and eleven years old?"

Well, we didn't. We had the same question, believe me. And, the State of California had questions of their own, especially since we didn't have any official school transcripts. So, we both took an eighth-grade equivalency test to officially graduate middle school and move on to high school. Ivana and I scored above average in every category, and started to explore our options for what we were going to do for high school.

There is one thing you need to know about my mom: she is an excellent and dedicated researcher. This led her to find a special-function correspondence school called American School. It catered to child actors, musicians, and athletes, as well as missionary families—students with the kind of schedules that preclude them from staying in one place for long. Graduates of the American School include Jessica Alba, the Osmond Brothers, Andre Agassi, and Bethany Hamilton.

As I filled out the portion on my application to American School that had to do with age, I wrote "almost eleven." So, it was understandable that the school had to look into the matter further and took their time before accepting Ivana and me as students. I do believe that, at the time, we held the record for the youngest students ever to enroll.

THE CESPEDES FAMILY

I wrote "almost eleven" on my high school application.

High school worked very much the same as elementary school. We would get up, grab our schoolbooks, go to our respective desks, and read and work through problems. The only thing was, now that we were in high school, Mom couldn't help us as much with our questions. So, we got a tutor when we really struggled, and worked through the material the rest of the time.

In high school, we took only one class at a time. This way, we could be hyper-focused on a subject, and spend as much time as we needed to understand the concepts and complete the exams. Our family was never too caught up in mastering every single subject. We knew that in our everyday lives, we weren't likely to need every specific fact we learned in subjects like geometry, biology, chemistry, sociology and British literature. Instead, we made sure we had a grasp on the lesson, and then we moved on to the next one.

Our approach was centered around proficiency rather than mastery of every subject and memorization of micro-details. We did recognize, however, that there were certain subjects that were important to master. These included writing, mathematics, anatomy, and business courses. We took our time with these classes to make sure that we really had them under our belt.

The last year of high school was pretty intense because we saw the end in sight, and were racing to get there. At this point, we were working ten hours a day, and finishing courses in two weeks.

I finished all my work for high school in January of 2011, at age thirteen. Of course, it took a little while longer to actually graduate because of the mailing, transcript, and final authorization processes.

Next came the topic on the mind of every teenage girl when they are preparing to graduate: prom. Yes, we did have a prom, and yes, we did go with our dad. Another thing you should know about my mom is that she is a gifted event planner. She helped us arrange our prom at a resort next to our house. We invited about forty friends, and had amazing food, lots of dancing, and plenty of fun.

The next year was what I like to call our gap year. Ivana and I were fifteen and fourteen at this point, and facing the dread of potentially having nothing to do. We had both graduated earlier than anticipated, and hadn't been planning on getting a job anytime soon. Now, we had a dilemma. Just waiting around, doing nothing was not an option for either of us.

Neither one of us had set the goal of getting a four-year degree and then using our degree to pursue an established career. We had always been more vocationally minded. Our thinking was that ten years of experience working in a certain profession would be far more valuable and worthwhile than the time it would take to first earn the degree, which we weren't sure really prepared us for the field. Now, we had to decide whether to start working at such a young age or go to college, after all.

THE CESPEDES FAMILY

Briana

When I was ten years old, I took the California Achievement Test (CAT) exam, to test my junior-high equivalency aptitude. I scored about average on every topic. Just like my sister Belicia, I remember writing on my application to high school "almost eleven" as my age.

After several months of correspondence with the school, in which I was required to verify my grades, aptitude and maturity level, I was accepted into American School of Correspondence. At the tender age of eleven, I finally began high school. Looking back on my early years of homeschooling, it's easy to see how I ended up on the accelerated track.

Even as a toddler, the smallest things like reading, tracing and math were incorporated into my daily schedule. The older girls were in their own grade so I would have my own book to complete. Some days I liked school but other days I would have much rather been outside. Once, I was very bored and didn't want to have to think or be challenged. So, I pretended not to be able to handwrite in cursive the letter A. Unfortunately for me, I was stuck on that for hours—but at least I didn't have to progress to the very difficult B!

When my sisters got old enough, they actually took on my mom's role and began teaching classes to us younger girls. I mentioned this earlier and how much I loved it. We learned math (Belicia taught that), science, character training, writing (taught by Ivana) and P.E. It was so much fun. I was the grade A favorite student, of course. (Just kidding, Giana!)

I never knew my favorite subjects in school and didn't really take time to pick one because I was generally good at them all. I'm more of a jack of all trades than a master of one. Mom always emphasized proficiency rather than mastery of the material before we were permitted to move on to the next book or grade. I believe that this is really fundamental to education, which is meant to be applied to real life. In real life, we don't remember every detail but we do know how to make educated choices.

Tips on How to Accelerate Your Own Education

☞ Do grades one through six at your student's own pace;

— It is important to get these foundations solid, so don't rush through. Move on when you're sure the student has a good grasp of it;

☞ Consider creating your own private school by filing your own private affidavit;

— This sounds scary but it entails filing a simple form online once a year. This gave us a great deal of flexibility. It also took away third-party deadlines and to-do's that would have distracted me from my first priority: discipleship. That is just me, of course. There are other moms who would have no problem under an umbrella and may even thrive. For us, it would have changed the heart of our homeschooling experience;

☞ Have your student take the eighth-grade equivalency exam when you think they are ready;

- If they score average to above average in all areas, start high school. If not, help them in the areas of weakness and then have them retake the exam;

☞ Select a high-school program that allows your student to go at their own pace;
☞ While your student is a junior in high school, consider having them also enroll at your local community college, no matter their age. Use your discretion as to whether or not you think they can handle both simultaneously;

- Start with a college class in which your student is likely to be successful;
- Online classes are a great option, since they are likely to feel similar to homeschooling;
- If your student wants to take a class on site, then consider taking the class with them the first time, especially if they are young;
- If possible, have siblings enroll in the same class together;
- Use your discretion when enrolling your student in classes in the social sciences. These classes sometimes entail classroom discussion topics your student may not be ready to handle;

☞ I highly recommend using CLEP exams as a student's final exam during their high school years, or sooner if you have an avid reader, or a student who is a good tester or really strong in a subject area of CLEP;

PRODUCTIVE HOMESCHOOLING

- CLEP offers over thirty different subject areas. If the student gets a passing score, they earn between three and twelve college credits;
- These credits can be banked for years. (It was twenty years, the last time I checked.) A student has twenty years to use these credits toward a college degree or potentially as an entrance to a non-APA law school;

☞ Especially if your student is very young, consider using a regionally accredited university that accepts CLEP credits and other credits by examination, ACE approved courses, portfolios, and other less conventional, less expensive and time-saving approaches to earning college credits;

☞ Help your student plan out their course of study very carefully;

☞ Pay close attention to university catalogues, course equivalencies, deadlines, due dates, academic counselors and such;

☞ Stay a couple of years ahead of your student so you can help them keep their momentum going; and

☞ Remember to check in with their hearts continuously, and make sure that this momentum and style of learning is best for them. You don't want your student to have regrets later, if you can help it (like my Briana did). I could have done a better job of this and worked harder at drawing out the silent journey some of their hearts were taking, specifically in the way they were experiencing pressure and wishing they could do things differently. Sometimes life allows you to intervene and head regrets off at the pass and sometimes it doesn't but love always moves us to try our best.

HOMESCHOOLING TIMELINE

Mama Vicki

We are often asked, "So, how did you do it? What did your home life look like at each stage of your daughters' lives?"

As I try to synthesize a myriad of memories into a concise picture of what our home life looked like, let me detail our primary focus for both character and academics at each stage of homeschooling.

It ended up working out in such a way that my girls completed their thirteen years of kindergarten through twelfth grade in eight years. Since they finished early, they were doing college work in the typical junior high-through-high school years. And, instead of taking general-education college courses, they were able to explore and develop their areas of aptitude and interest.

PRODUCTIVE HOMESCHOOLING

Ages Birth to Three Years

(Some of what follows will be a recap of material found earlier in the book. I recap it here so you can get a sense of our homeschool timeline.)

When the girls were between the ages of infancy and three years, we focused on teaching them the following character traits:

- ☞ Obedience right away, all the way and in a happy way;
- ☞ A happy heart—the absence of grumbling and the presence of gratitude; and
- ☞ The beginnings of self-control, including things like being able to sit in a highchair for minutes at a time. I started at one minute and slowly increased the time to thirty minutes as the girls started to read.

Our academic focus during these years included the following:

- ☞ Simple ABC's, numbers to 100, and the proper way to hold a pencil and write their name;
- ☞ Basic phonics and reading; and
- ☞ Lots of reading to the child.

Things were kept pretty simple during these years, primarily because we had a baby in 1996, 1997, 1998, 2000 (and then later in 2010, but that is another story).

I loved being pregnant because of the precious gift that God was giving us, but pregnancy didn't seem to like me

THE CESPEDES FAMILY

much. Instead of morning sickness, I had all-day sickness and could often be found in the bathroom, on my knees, violently vomiting.

It was hard to be up, to cook, or to do most anything that required the use of my mind but somehow, we got through it. In looking back, I wouldn't change it for the world. It was humbling in all the right places and God's good work was at hand. Somehow, He gave me the strength to press on with the discipleship of my girls, no matter how sick I felt.

I knew I wanted to homeschool my girls but I had no idea how to go about it. So, I saw my opportunity to practice while the girls were tiny. Being my firstborn daughter, Ivana became my faithful and endearing guinea pig. She was the first to experience everything that I was trying out.

As soon as Ivana could sit in a highchair, I would sit her down and sing songs, read her the Bible, and recite simple Scriptures to her. I usually chose Scriptures that were in line with her character training. For example, Scriptures containing messages like these: *Do all things without grumbling*...

PRODUCTIVE HOMESCHOOLING

Children, obey your parents in the Lord for this is right...A happy heart makes good medicine.

I bought a few supplies at garage sales to teach Ivana the letters, numbers, colors, shapes, days of the week—whatever I could find. And I bought her a few pencils and crayons so she could learn to scribble.

We did this every morning, with Ivana in the highchair and Belicia growing in my belly. To my amazement, Ivana started to learn these simple things when she was tiny. I thought, *I must have a genius for a child!*

I kept going, recognizing those moments when she was ready to progress. Once Belicia was born, I would put her in her car seat next to Ivana and me during lesson times and then, when she was big enough, in her highchair.

Sometimes I would let Ivana pretend to teach Belicia the things she knew. Well, much sooner than expected, Belicia started to answer simple questions I was asking Ivana! The same thing happened when Briana was tiny, as she started to answer simple questions I was asking Belicia.

I soon realized, *Wait a minute...my children aren't geniuses after all! Children just have an amazing capacity to learn and are generally underestimated.*

By the age of three, all three girls were able to read simple books and count to 100-plus. They were able to comprehend and accomplish things I thought were beyond the capacity of a three-year-old.

It is true that some children have learning disabilities, but their capacity to learn is beyond what we might expect from them too. As she discloses in her own words in this book, Giana was diagnosed with severe dyslexia and dysgraphia. This caused her to struggle with reading, writing, spelling, penmanship—pretty much everything having to do with the written word. In every area not impacted by her learning disability, she shone, despite being tiny. I was surprised and thrilled by Giana's capacity to exceed my expectations.

Ages 4 thru 8th grade

When the girls were four years old and continuing through eighth grade, the focus was on gradually increasing the duration of teaching sessions and adding various subjects. Otherwise, the approach was generally the same.

Thankfully, by this time I was done being pregnant for a while. So, I was able to start a little co-op at our house. We had fifteen children as students, and mommies who would share teaching responsibilities and teach according to their strengths. Between the mommies and the students, we made many new friends. This was a fun season that included lots and lots of play dates, slumber parties, field trips, celebrations, pizza parties, movie nights—you name it.

During these years, we would typically start out with our time of devotion. This centered around Bible reading, prayer, Scripture memorization, and songs. Then we would move into approximately two hours of academics. Usually by lunchtime, we were done with academic school.

At lunchtime, the girls would eat and then play outside for no less than an hour. Sometimes playtime lasted much longer, especially if I saw that they were involved in creative play—creating something tangible like a fort, a short film, a play, and so on. I loved seeing spontaneous initiative and creativity so, whenever possible, I would let them play much longer during those creative play times.

PRODUCTIVE HOMESCHOOLING

The afternoons were usually dedicated to a quiet time. This time was set aside for napping or, for those who weren't tired, reading and journaling.

The girls all knew that quiet time was usually followed by an outing of some kind, where we often went to visit someone. This was one of my favorite times of day because it afforded us opportunities to put truth and love into action.

I loved to focus on being of love and service to anyone, and particularly widows, orphans, the sick, the poor, and the men and women in military service. On Wednesdays, we visited with the seniors of Placerita Bible Church. They allowed the girls to sing and recite Scripture to them and share anything they wanted to share.

The girls hugged the seniors, visited with them and loved them like grandparents. We often celebrated the girls' birthdays with the seniors. One year, Belicia invited all the seniors to our house for dinner. She and her friends cooked dinner for them and served them like waitresses.

While we often found ways to serve outside the home, we also taught the girls that service right in their own home is of primary importance. Service at home included working hard on their chores, being kind and respectful, being grateful, doing special things for each other, and working on good relationships with those at home. Interestingly, being of service to one's own family can sometimes be harder than serving outside the home, but it is just as important.

We also spent time on what I called proactive training. This involved helping the girls to learn and practice right responses to things they were struggling with currently or might be struggling with the following year. When the girls were tiny, proactive training included practicing responding to the directives "come" and "stop." When they were older, they practiced the proper response to someone at college offering them drugs. They also practiced the proper response to a man who might ask them out on a date, under the belief that they were older than their actual age.

I remembered being young and struggling to know the right thing to do in a given situation. I really wanted to make obedience and wise living as easy as possible for my girls. I felt that this was of even greater importance due to the fact that they were engaged in adult studies and activities at such a young age. No matter how mature they seemed to be, I never lost sight of the fact that they were still young and lacked life experience. I wanted to help them as much as I could while I was there to offer guidance. Soon enough, they would be out on their own and making their own choices and decisions.

Looking Ahead Toward College and Vocation

Mama Vicki

Because all my girls were pretty young as they neared high school, I was unsure of our next step. I knew how important the high school years would be in terms of vocational and collegiate possibilities, and the girls' pursuit of a path that would be meaningful and fulfilling to them. I was watchful of each girl, trying to get a sense of their aptitudes and leanings.

I had developed the habit of staying a couple of years ahead. In this way, I was able to keep from stunting their progress and momentum by having to hit the pause button at each crossroads. I knew the time had come to start researching high schools. I was looking for schools that might work well with our philosophy of education, encourage independent learning, and give the girls freedom to go at their own pace while still abiding by state guidelines.

High School Years

Mama Vicki

By the time the girls reached their high school years, I felt that most of them were ready for more independent learning and a gradual distancing from me as their teacher. I knew that they were eventually going to need to be comfortable being completely independent from me. Seeing their rate of acceleration, I realized it was going to be sooner rather than later.

As preparation for the time when the girls would find themselves completely independent, we decided to approach high school as independent study. The girls would be taking care of all their assignments and exams, and dealing with the submissions, course requests, and the like.

As it turned out, they rarely asked for my help. I had an eye out for opportunities to help them arrange internships, meetings, and field trips intended to expand their scope of subject experience and exploration in areas of interest to them.

When I did my research, I found a special-function high school that met all of our criteria. The school had a solid history of accreditation, and was geared towards military families and celebrity kids who couldn't attend conventional public or private school. It was unique in that it allowed students to take courses at home at their own pace. It also allowed the girls to take a college preparatory pathway just in case they elected to go to college.

Since the girls were all pretty young when they started high school—certainly much younger than most high school students—they had to obtain permission from the school to submit their applications, and provide verification of eighth grade equivalency via national examination. So, they did, and they were all accepted. Each one scored average or above average nationally for all students completing the eighth grade in all subjects.

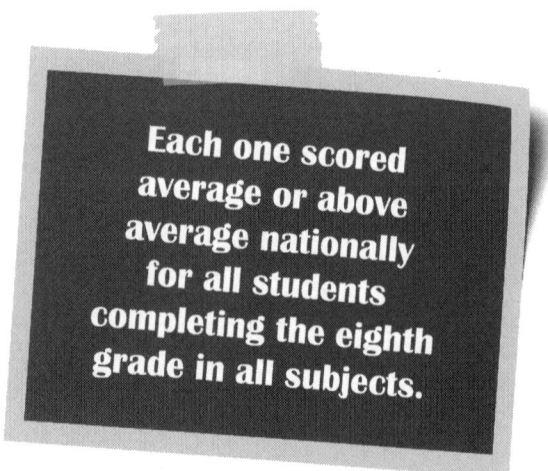

The school allowed their students to do one course at a time or multiple courses. We opted to do one course at a time so that the girls could really focus, become proficient in the material, and determine whether any interest or unusual aptitudes were ignited by the subject matter.

When the girls wanted or needed to learn a specific skill, I tried to find a way to help them learn it. Or, I helped them connect with someone who used that skill professionally, so they could request the opportunity to shadow them and see what the application of the skill looked like in a real-world business setting. We wanted them to get hands-on experience whenever possible.

PRODUCTIVE HOMESCHOOLING

During this time, I began to bring in tutors for subjects in which I was weak, like the higher math and sciences. I really enjoyed seeing how those relationships further encouraged my daughters' learning. It was also encouraging to hear that the tutors saw focus, diligence and a desire for excellence in the girls, regardless of their affinity for the subject matter. All my girls were open and eager to learn.

Jan declared Sunday nights Book Night and we started a tradition of family devotion on Sunday evenings. We would gather together after dinner and each person would share something that they were studying, give a summary of a book they read, or share what God had been teaching them that week. We also shared praises, prayer requests, and schedules for the upcoming week, and asked forgiveness from each other for anything that was not yet resolved. Finally, Papa would give us a Bible lesson and encourage us to follow after God and His truth.

This tradition is a precious one that none of us will forget because of the blessing and impact it has had on our lives as individuals and as a family. Many of our girls have expressed a desire to continue this tradition with their own families one day, Lord willing. Thank you, Jan, for this amazing gift.

OUR SURPRISE BLESSING

Meet Eliana

Mama Vicki

Around the time that many of the girls were finishing up high school, we announced to them the wonderful news that we were pregnant. Several months later, we lost the baby—our third glory baby that God took early for reasons only He knows. It was a painful loss. Thankfully, God used the loss of our previous two children to teach me that He was motivated by His perfect love, kindness and mercy in allowing this to happen.

Less than a year later, at the end of 2009, God allowed us to conceive. What a profound and joyful blessing. Once again, I experienced what I had come to think of as my usual all-day-all-pregnancy sickness. I got severely nauseous and had trouble keeping down my food.

Given that I was forty by this time and we had recently lost a baby, I was on bedrest for many months. I had to keep my body in a tilted position on a recliner so I would have a chance of keeping down food for my growing baby.

I am not quite sure how schooling continued during this time. All I can say is that I am grateful that the girls were independent learners by then. God allowed this baby to live and on October 20th, 2010, I gave birth to Eliana Hope Cespedes. She was ten years, three months younger than Giana, my fourth daughter. That was quite a gap.

Little Ellie, as we called her, was a blessing from the moment she was conceived. She instantly had five mommies (me and her four sisters). We all adored her and were invested in her good and the discipleship of her soul and educating of her mind.

I appreciated the honesty of my older girls when I asked them to share with me the areas of their upbringing that they felt I could have improved upon, changed, or thrown out altogether. They shared their truths in a gracious and gentle way, and with so much gratitude and charity, they moved me to tears.

In homeschooling Ellie, I am seeking to take the best of what was done with my older girls and avoid anything unhelpful or unproductive. Our goals are still the same but the method may be slightly different. After all, she arrived in a very different season of our family's life, and in some ways is like an only child. She is my only student at the moment and does not have the benefit of a built-in peer system comprised of her sisters. They are all adult women now, out in the world and the workplace. So, I am always on the lookout for opportunities to connect Ellie with other children on a regular basis.

It is important for me to continue learning how to improve as a homeschool mommy. I believe that seeking to be better at anything is right and good. It is incredibly significant that I am the steward of someone who is more precious to me than anything in the world. I know that the efforts we make today to build Ellie's young mind and heart will become a contribution that yields fruit for her lifetime.

For all you parents out there, regardless of whether you homeschool or not, I want to say that every effort you make to be a good steward of those precious gifts God has given you in your home matters and is significant. Do not grow weary in doing good.

My youngest is now eight years old and thriving. She is a great little student, full of curiosity and energy. Jan and I pray that we will be good stewards of the precious moments we have with her, and we pray to do an even better job of homeschooling Ellie than we did with her sisters.

At the very moment that I am writing this, Ellie is bringing to life an imaginative story, crawling under the blankets of my bed and using pillows as the characters. In the midst of this, she stops to recount stories, answer my questions about what she thinks learning means and her definition of school. She is still in her jammies and her hair is floating, due to static in the air. She is quite an amusing and heartwarming sight.

PRODUCTIVE HOMESCHOOLING

Ellie's Daily Schedule

Ellie's daily schedule is below. Additionally, we are always on the lookout for unscheduled teachable moments. We try to stay intentional with choices we make related to how Ellie should spend her time.

- ✓ 7:30 to 8:00 a.m. Good morning snuggle, which lasts as long as possible;
- ✓ Prayer and Bible time with Mama;
- ✓ Breakfast and chores;
- ✓ 9:30 Sit-down school time;
- ✓ 11:30 Lunchtime and outside free play;
- ✓ 1:00 p.m. Reading or rest hour;
- ✓ 2:00 p.m.:

☞ Opportunities for service

— Visiting seniors, as well as the sick, lonely, or grieving;

☞ Nurturing relationships;

— Time with Papa, sisters, and friends; and

☞ Co-op classes in the community, etc.

Ellie

I am glad we homeschool because my mommy is my teacher and she loves me and is nice to me. I get to play outside on my breaks and do classes like zoo school and farm school

THE CESPEDES FAMILY

with other kids who are homeschooled. So, even though I'm homeschooled, I get to have some friends too. I also have friends who go to school and I play with them on Saturdays, Sundays and school breaks.

I like to learn because learning is fun, especially in homeschool. I get to do lots of things like swimming, classes, baking, trips, slumber parties, spending time with friends, snuggling in the morning with my mama and giving her some sugar kisses, doing math in my jammies and being around my big sisters.

I have so many favorite things about homeschooling, I am going to have to make a list for you:

- Building forts in my house;
- Cleaning while we sing and dance to TobyMac or the music from Hamilton (the play);
- Reading and laughing with Mama in our big smushy chair in the library;
- Climbing on my play set;
- Movie nights;
- Being part of ESCAPE (a community theater group);
- Gymnastics camps;
- Doing my first Spartan race;
- Vacation Bible school;
- Songs of Summer voice camp;
- Play days with friends;
- Farm school;
- Art classes;
- Visiting seniors;
- Taking food to people when they are sick or just lost somebody, like a family who lost their papa or a baby;
- Dropping off surprise gifts;
- Piano and voice lessons with my sister Ivana;
- Sign language with my sister Giana;

PRODUCTIVE HOMESCHOOLING

- Buying old books at the thrift store;
- Playing UNO and chess with my neighbors Malayna and Jacob;
- Golfing and riding bikes with my papa;
- Math class with Miss Ashley; and
- Studying history in Philadelphia and in Williamsburg, visiting the homes of George Washington, Thomas Jefferson, Thomas Edison, and Albert Einstein, and dressing up with a special dress and bonnet like they used to wear and eating the kind of food they used to eat. (I can't wait to go back.)

CONSIDERING COLLEGE AND ALTERNATIVES

Feeling Out of Step with My Sisters

Briana

When high school came around in 2008, I was only ten years old. I was excited to be in a regular routine and start something new. I remember lingering over the fresh pages of my psychology textbook. I wanted to do everything right, like a good high school student. Given how young I was at the time, I started out slowly.

It took me the longest to finish my first subject because I was intent on really learning it. Then I noticed how my sisters finished each of their subjects in so little time, and I wanted to do the same. So, I compromised. Instead of learning the way I learn best—slowly, steadily, structurally—I changed my goal from learning a subject to finishing it.

PRODUCTIVE HOMESCHOOLING

That was a mistake. I discovered that I am different than my sisters in this regard. I don't seem to have the same ability retain and absorb the material unless I take my time. I don't do well when I am rushed.

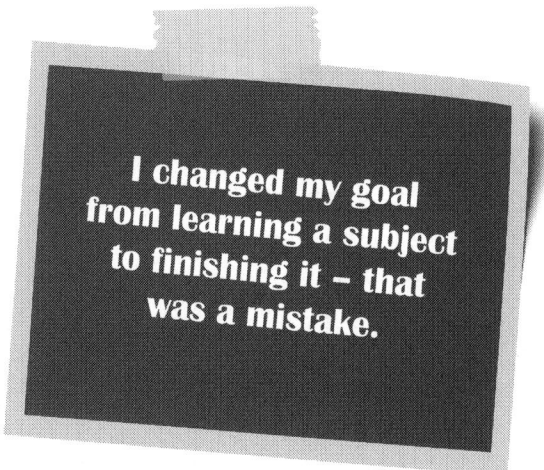

I changed my goal from learning a subject to finishing it – that was a mistake.

My sisters seemed to learn best when they focused hard for a few hours but I needed a few days or even weeks. I didn't realize until later that this didn't make me any less capable mentally for academic or real-life success; it was simply indicative of the fact that I had a different way of learning. I would have to hear something, then read it, then hear a story told about it before I could commit it to memory. If I could get my hands on it, I'd do even better.

I remember hating geometry so much that I actually failed it. The school didn't accept a failing grade, so I had to retake the course. No matter how hard I tried, I could not understand geometry, and it made me feel terrible. Belicia was tutoring me through it, and I felt so stupid much of the time because I simply couldn't get it. I couldn't understand why it came so easily to her but not to me.

THE CESPEDES FAMILY

I wanted to finish it so badly. There I would be, coming up with the answer to the length of a base of a triangle for example, thinking to myself, *I'll soon be over this huge mountain I have to cross!*

Biology was another difficult class. I remember fungus and hypothesis, and that's about it. Then there were courses I loved. My favorite course was Planning Your Career. I've always loved thinking about the future, and would get excited when I talked about the prospect of going to work, having coworkers, and joining the nine-to-five work force. I love the idea of work.

I also loved career planning because I found it fun to try to figure out what career path would be a match for my personality and skill sets. I was endlessly amazed by the vast array of potential careers.

Overall, high school was an overwhelmingly rapid experience, but a necessary one. I knew I needed to finish it in order to comply with state law and be free to go on to learn things I really loved. I graduated at thirteen years old.

I have since wondered what my life would have been like if I were public-schooled, and I probably will always wonder. I'm a hard worker and I think I would have excelled in public school.

Elementary homeschooling was great because it helped to inform my character, convictions, study habits and perceptions of the world. It was a foundation. For high school, however, getting up early and learning under the structured teaching of a professor who was gradually explaining material over a semester would have been my preference. I would have preferred a set schedule where I got up in the morning with a purpose, and left the house to go to school.

You know how people always wish they could be homeschooled so they could sleep in and do homework in their pajamas? Well, as far as I'm concerned, that should be reserved for Saturdays.

PRODUCTIVE HOMESCHOOLING

College Alternatives

Mama Vicki

As soon as Ivana and Belicia started high school, I began to research options for possible steps after high school. I looked into college options, trying to determine whether there were ways for my girls, who were not yet even teenagers, to do college at home.

I also considered many options for the girls beyond the usual college track. These included vocational training, internships, volunteering, alternative pathways to law, serving with missionary families we knew all over the world, and letting the girls spend a good amount of time with, and learn from, women who were gifted in various areas—essentially an in-home apprenticeship.

During that time, I bumped into a book about accelerated distance learning. The book introduced me to some viable options that excited me. First, I needed to watch my girls and see what their unique passions and skill sets were, and how they learned in terms of interests and goals.

It was a bonus that my husband happened to be an entrepreneur and business owner. We were able to regularly include the girls in Jan's ventures. The girls were able to go to the office and help with some basic tasks like bookkeeping, filing, cleaning, and phone calls. Jan gave the girls such great support and encouraged them to start their own companies, be entrepreneurs, and reach for the stars.

Papa Jan

I know that Vicki and the girls identify me as an entrepreneur, a mover and shaker, and a man with a vision. If and when God blesses the vision, I move forward with all the energy and skill that I possess.

This is one of the most important principles I believe my girlies have learned: that entrepreneurship is something to take advantage of in this country, and that there are rewards to reap by all who put in the effort and earn the knowledge to attain their goals.

Identifying a Path Forward

Briana

All throughout high school, and even more so in community college, I felt my desires growing and began to think about what I wanted to do with my life. I fervently asked God and my family what I should do. It was such a big question to be asking at only fourteen years of age. I knew that I wanted to work hard and conquer the world but that was about it. I had no idea what avenue I wanted to pursue or how to contribute to society rather than take from it.

When I was fifteen years old, I decided to take a step into an arena I had always been curious about, and began exploring firefighter training. I loved meeting and getting to personally know the firefighters, and I loved every second of what was essentially paramilitary training.

Twice a month, my Saturdays were greatly uplifted by firefighter training. We did everything from challenging workouts, community service, belaying ladders, and working through obstacles while blindfolded. I loved keeping up with the guys, sweating hard during the training, and racing with the turnouts, all with my brothers in training.

During firefighter training, I learned a lot about myself, especially about the kind of person I respected and wanted to be myself. From that moment on, I knew that I wanted to be involved in some kind of public service. When I thought back to how my family had always called me the police officer of the family, I realized that my career path had always been inside of me, waiting to reveal itself.

I could not enlist quite yet. I was still a bit too young. I had graduated high school in December of 2011 and gotten my diploma at only thirteen years old.

Marking the Milestones

Mama Vicki

As the girls finished high school, I wanted to make sure they didn't miss out on a prom-like experience. They were all only thirteen or younger at the time, so we did a formal father-daughter ball at a beautiful golf club resort and invited twenty of their closest friends. We took formal pictures and had a fancy dinner with dancing and a special speech given by Jan, Ivana and Belicia.

We also took senior pictures and planned to celebrate their accomplishment with a home graduation with friends and family.

Doing College from Home

Mama Vicki

By the time the girls finished high school, it had become clear to me that college was going to be the next step for the girls after all, due to their ages and interests. I had discovered that there was a way for the girls to work toward a college degree without having to move away. Best of all, it also allowed them to structure their studies in such a way that they could proceed at their own pace.

I learned about The Big Three regionally accredited universities—Thomas Edison State College, Excelsior, and Charter Oak State College—that recognized credits earned from courses taken at regionally accredited institutions approved by the American Council on Education, and/or credits earned by examination.

This opened up a world of possibilities. So, I set to work out potential pathways for each daughter, based upon her area of interest and her end goal. It went something like this:

- Identify area of study or end goal that daughter wants to pursue/ achieve;
- Identify specific college and degree that will allow her to pursue area of study and qualify her to achieve her end goal;
- Get a detailed list for the degree's specific course-credit distribution;
- Work with the local community college to determine course equivalency;
- Look to see which CLEP exams or ACE courses could also satisfy some of the required courses;
- Replace as many of the required courses as possible with community college courses, CLEP and ACE courses to keep costs down;
- Apply for admission to Big Three college of choice, write letter of appeal to dean and submit high school and community college transcripts;
- Take a look at academic evaluation and do a more finely-tuned plan for course equivalency;

☞ Once all or nearly all course equivalency credits are earned, enroll in university and complete any needed credits required for the degree; and
☞ Graduate for a fraction of the cost, usually in less time.

This is the way we handled bachelor's degrees for Ivana, Belicia and Briana. Giana has recently graduated with her Bachelor's in ASL Interpreting. It was a degree not offered by any of the Big Three, so she has taken a different route and is loving it.

Exploring Community College

Mama Vicki

Meanwhile, we talked to the girls about exploring areas of interest at the local community college while they finished up their high school. They took culinary classes, French, Italian, sciences, accounting, and more. (Ivana realized she loved sciences.)

Belicia really liked bookkeeping and wanted to pursue accounting. At her dad's encouragement, she became certified, even before she graduated high school. Given that the interest was there, it made sense that maybe she should try an accounting course at our local college.

Frankly, we were not sure how well she would do, given her age. It took some time for the local college to give her the green light to enroll at such a young age. Once they realized that she was a junior at her accredited high school, they agreed to accept her.

THE CESPEDES FAMILY

To our surprise, Belicia not only loved her class, she excelled at it. Her professor stated that she was the top student in her class, going beyond what he expected or asked of her.

Meanwhile, Briana took her love for public service and appreciation of law and politics and became part of our local Fire Explorer Program.

During Giana's period of considering and trying various paths and options, she took her first ASL course. She quickly discovered that it was something she loved and wanted to pursue after high school.

Belicia

Beginning in January of 2012, Ivana and I decided to start taking classes for the winter semester at our local community college, College of the Canyons (COC). I believe that, once again, we set a record for youngest students there. For a while, we simply took classes that we thought were fun, like languages, cooking and tennis. (It wasn't long before I became very competitive in my tennis game.) We also joined a collegiate choir at a local university. And I started to explore the computer world in programming and audio technology at College of the Canyons.

Both Ivana and I love to learn and had trained ourselves to enjoy the constant stretching and challenging of our minds. So, we soon realized that we needed to stop taking classes just for enjoyment and begin to truly study something.

I have always been a daddy's girl. So, when I started to consider what I might want to study, I naturally thought of the time I spent at my dad's office. Dad owns a landscaping construction company called International Environmental Corporation and happens to be a very visionary entrepreneur. He is constantly exploring business prospects and often has his hands in a new business deal.

PRODUCTIVE HOMESCHOOLING

From time to time, I went to the office with Dad and played the role of his secretary. I helped him write checks, listened to his latest business ideas, watched him fiddle in the stock market, and worked with his bookkeeper. I even helped fix his electronics and traveled with him to his work sites.

I loved going to work with Dad. It was precious time we got to spend together, and it was a great introduction to the world of business. Thanks to that time spent in Dad's office, I knew that I enjoyed the business world and more specifically, the finance side of things. Since I felt so drawn to finance, I decided to start studying bookkeeping.

Giana

In the Fall of 2012, I was a twelve-year-old, first-year college student at College of the Canyons. I took my first class, Safety and Sanitation, with all three of my sisters. I had never set foot on a campus before, except to attend someone else's graduation. When I tried to imagine what a classroom would be like, I envisioned classroom scenes from T.V. and movies.

I will never forget my first day of class. I was so nervous, I was shaking. I had no idea what to expect. All I knew was that I would, of course, have a teacher and be surrounded by students several years older than I. My sisters were trying to encourage me by telling me how the class worked and what to expect.

I ended up loving the professor but when he got up in front of the room and started talking, he totally lost me. While he was explaining what would be required of us in class, he used terminology I had never heard before.

"Come up and get your syllabus," he said.

Syllabus? I was thinking. *What's a syllabus?*

My sisters all looked at me expectantly and said, "Go up and get one!"

THE CESPEDES FAMILY

As I nervously went up to the front of the class, two other students followed but there was only one syllabus left.

"The rest of you can pull it up on Blackboard," said the professor.

Normally, I would have let one of the other two have it. But I had no idea what Blackboard was or how to access it. So, pulling it up on Blackboard wasn't an option for me. I clenched my jaw, grabbed the paper and ran back to my sisters. They must have all wondered why I was breathing so heavily.

That same day, our professor asked us to come to the front of the class and tell everyone about our favorite cuisine—whatever that meant. Thankfully, I had three sisters go up before me, and that was enough time for me to figure out the meaning of the word cuisine. (My favorite cuisine was Italian.)

These are just a few of the bumbling—and humbling!—moments I experienced in my very first class. Yeah, it was awkward and uncomfortable for a little bit, but eventually I got the hang of it and felt completely integrated into classroom life.

THE GIRLS' COLLEGE EXPERIENCES

Ivana

I remember being about to leave the house to take a particularly challenging CLEP exam (College Level Examination Program) when Mom informed me that my school had cut my program and forgotten to tell me. The semester started the following week.

After a quick moment to gather my thoughts and take a deep breath, I responded, "Okay, Mom, what's next?"

This response could only have come from a heart that trusted God's work. At that moment in time, I did not question what He was doing. In fact, for a brief moment, a strong feeling of excitement filled my heart for what was to come next. That's true hope, and that attitude has rescued me in many other instances of grief, surprise and difficulty. I also credit homeschooling with my measured reaction to that disappointment. Homeschooling me gave my parents the necessary time to train me to be adaptable in every situation.

THE CESPEDES FAMILY

(Incidentally, I ended up getting one of the highest scores on that CLEP exam.)

Over the next few years, I put my heart and mind to work. I graduated college with a 4.0 GPA in Natural Sciences, lost over thirty pounds, restored my health, went abroad to study at Oxford, somehow managed to write an eighty-four-page thesis in two months, received my Master's in Health Science with a 3.98 GPA, and spent the greatest year of my life working as a production assistant at a recording studio in Los Angeles.

How many people get to say that Verdine White of *Earth, Wind & Fire* decided to call himself by his full name so that no one would confuse his name with my nickname, Vi? Meeting people like Sergio Mendes, Scott Mayo, DJ Khalid, RZA, Chicago, Kiss, and many others inspired the musicality in me. Over the past six months, I have been involved in several cool projects, including singing for The Grammy's, The Disney Channel, and a Nike commercial. And, I have met many incredible session musicians who have become dear friends.

Belicia

We decided to test the waters to make sure that accounting was the right direction for me. Along these lines, I took an accounting class in the Spring of 2012 towards an associate's degree at College of the Canyons (COC), the community college.

You would think I was a little out of my league. After all, I was a fourteen-year-old, ex-homeschooler just exploring career options, and suddenly I was going for a difficult major with an eighteen-unit load composed of accounting, business law, economics, and a few other business classes. My family and I, however, were excited to discover that I was aptly prepared and very comfortable at COC. We attributed this to one thing: my homeschool education for all the years prior.

PRODUCTIVE HOMESCHOOLING

The focus of college education is primarily independent study rather than classroom learning, and there is naturally a greater weight of personal responsibility in college than in high school. Little did I know during my many years of being homeschooled that I was being equipped for this learning style. It wasn't until I entered college that I realized the true value of the habitual self-study produced by homeschooling.

That was the first time I had experienced the real pressure of having to study, take exams, and finish the homework for a permanent grade. I couldn't have foreseen it, but it was the first time I would have to stay up past midnight for a reason other than parties or birthdays.

The pressure and deadlines helped me, so I was surprised to learn that very few of my fellow students felt the same way. I took every quiz seriously, every assignment as an urgent 'to do.' That's where my years of independent study set me apart. Completing the various projects was like solving a complex puzzle and I thoroughly enjoyed it. The material clicked with me and I excelled in my accounting class.

My professor noticed. He knew I would do everything in my power to not simply get an A in the class, but be as close to 100% as I could. He knew that I would finish the homework every day, do the extra-credit problems, and read the assigned chapters as well as the recommended chapters for the next day's class.

He quickly found out how old I was and assumed I was a dual-enrollment high school student for most of the semester, like every other minor at COC. Eventually he discovered that I was a high school graduate in my first semester of college.

"Well, I was homeschooled," I explained.

"That explains *everything*," he said with a grin. "I've never seen anyone so young who understood the materials so quickly. And I've never had a high-school-age student *even finish* this class, much less finish first. I really encourage you to continue pursuing accounting!"

That class gave me a lot of confidence. I was excited for the next challenge—Accounting II in the summer of 2012. I did even better in this class. The material was tougher, but I had already tested myself and passed. At this point, I not only knew I could finish the class, I knew I could finish well.

My professor was again impressed that I finished first, especially after finding out my age and the other classes I was taking in my full load.

I am not saying this to puff myself up. I recognize that for every strength God has given me, I have ten times as many weaknesses. But I do want to encourage you readers. I want you to know that doing well in your academics is completely possible, even in unlikely situations. Yes, it takes hard work and dedication to sit down and teach yourself a concept you don't yet understand. And yes, it takes sacrifice and concentration to stretch your mind. But let me tell you, *it is worth it!*

By the winter of 2012, when I was fifteen years old, my parents and I had come to the conclusion that I was blessed in academics, discipline, and accounting concepts. So, we determined that I should go for a full, four-year, Bachelor's Degree in Accounting. We also knew, however, that I was not going to be able to go away to college. I didn't even have a driver's permit yet. The only local university that was even an option cost far more than we could afford.

That's when Mom began her research. She found a university—Thomas Edison State College—with a regionally accredited online program. They accepted units from practically any outside institution, as long as it was recognized and accredited. That meant that they would accept all of the community college classes I had taken, as well as other distance-learning units like the glorious CLEP (College Level Examination Program).

PRODUCTIVE HOMESCHOOLING

CLEP is essentially like an AP test in that it gives students a certain amount of college credits if passed. CLEPs are administered by The College Board, a national testing agency that keeps an accredited transcript of all CLEP units in a testing bank for up to twenty years. These accredited units can be used at practically any college or university to satisfy prerequisite requirements, general-education units, and even upper division classes. CLEPs cover a huge array of subjects from general sciences such as anatomy, to very specific fields such as human resources management.

A student will study independently for as long as it takes to prepare for the test, using any study program of their choice. Some use the CLEP text study guides, others use college textbooks, still others get tutoring or use online exam study prep resources.

Testing centers for these CLEPs, and a similar testing program called DSST (Dante's Exams, usually for military), are located at many colleges and tutoring centers. We took all of our CLEPs and DSSTs at the Master's College in Santa Clarita. This campus felt like our second home at a point because of our endless visits to obtain those units.

In the month of December of 2012, I did nothing but eat, sleep, and take CLEP tests and more CLEP tests. In that one month, I completed a total of sixty units in community-college classes, online classes, and these credit-by-examination tests. There were weeks during that month when I spent at least twelve hours a day in what we called The CLEP room.

THE CESPEDES FAMILY

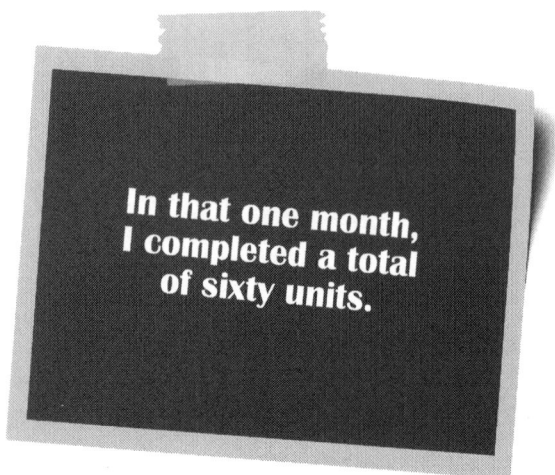

In that one month, I completed a total of sixty units.

This was the first time I really had to sacrifice for academics. I remember how I struggled to maintain the level of discipline needed to reach my goals. Some days I would have internal conversations with myself, rationalizing, *I'm still a kid! I need at least a little free time to play tennis, go to evening church services, and relax.*

Then I would look up at my Path to Degree board, where we had listed the courses and exams I needed to take, as well as the number of units I needed to graduate. Every time I finished a course or passed a CLEP exam, I got to mark it off with red ink. I got a great sense of satisfaction as I watched the number of units needed to graduate getting lower and lower. That difficult period of hyperintensity was thankfully brief.

At the end of 2012, I applied to Thomas Edison State College (TESC)—a college set up to be a distance-learning college for older adults trying to finish up their degrees. I was told that, because of my age, I was not allowed to apply without permission. I had to submit a letter of appeal to the dean of the college, requesting permission to apply. I also had to provide verification that I was capable of not only handling the requirements of a four-year regionally accredited university with high standards, but succeeding.

As proof, I submitted my community college transcript as well as my College Board transcripts. Based on these, I was given permission to apply. Shortly after the application process, I was accepted and ready to enroll. In February of 2013, I enrolled in the Bachelors of Science in Business Administration/Accounting/CPA program at Thomas Edison State College.

At this point, we decided to prepare for the possibility of me going all the way with accounting. Mom had mapped out all of the requirements for the degree, as well as the additional requirements to earn my CPA license. We used that map to determine which CLEPs (and other online classes) I would take, which community college classes would transfer, and what units I had left to complete.

By the time I was accepted at TESC, I only had to complete seven more classes to finish my degree. These were all of my upper-division accounting classes like Auditing I and II, Income Taxation, and Advanced Accounting. These classes were the most difficult, mind-stretching projects I had taken on. I stayed up passed midnight more than a few times in order to finish and submit assignments.

Thankfully, I was able to do pretty well on all these assignments, and ended up with only one B+ on my college transcript. After two, twelve-week semesters at TESC, in July of 2013, I was able to graduate with my Bachelor of Science in Business Administration (BSBA) in Accounting/CPA.

Briana

I began in the local community college as soon as I passed the entrance exams. My experience at College of the Canyons was wonderful. I was trained all the way through math by a professor who *loved* math and that made such a difference to me. I could now relate when my friends would tell me how much they loved their favorite teachers, and how they influenced their students to be better, shoot higher and dream bigger. My heart went out to my friends when they complained about teachers who seemed like they didn't care about the material or the students themselves.

I took statistics and excelled there. I took cooking classes, interior design, health science, English and more. Being in the classroom was such a new and exciting experience for me and it taught me how I learn best—with time, guidance, examples and practice.

Once my classmates would find out my age, they freaked out every single time. I remember one guy refused to stop calling me a prodigy for months. Ironically, this so-called prodigy had to go home and look up the meaning of the word.

You might ask, "How did you handle college-level work at thirteen years old?"

I don't really know. Attending college with students eight years older than me, taking difficult math classes and doing well, and earning a college degree were all things I never could have imagined myself doing at that age. Then again, I have always liked pushing myself—a mentality I learned from my time in homeschool as a student encouraged to learn independently of everyone around me.

I was terrified and intimidated at first but adjusted quickly. I eventually came to love it. My sisters did it, so I knew I could too. It was hard at times but when I put in the work, I got it done and did well, regardless of the subject. I learned a great deal and made many memories.

I always got along with the professors and worked hard to ask them good questions. My goal was to get an A on every test. I saw the A as a challenge and so I worked for it. And, because I shot high, I got there. I never missed an opportunity to earn extra credit. I knew it was hugely important for any student wanting a good grade, not to mention assured favor from the professor. Too often, I saw my classmates give up before they had even begun.

I spent two years at COC, working though my general-education requirements and taking fun classes. After COC, I started to make plans. I knew I wanted a bachelor's degree, so I got a general degree in liberal arts with an emphasis in business from Thomas Edison State College. I saw it as a stepping stone to a higher degree. I liked business and was raised with it so I thought I should pursue an MBA.

In March of 2014 when I was fifteen years old, I graduated from Thomas Edison. My older sisters and I were blessed to be able to travel to the actual university campus in New Jersey for the graduation ceremony. It was an incredible experience to be able to walk the stage with the other graduates, hear our names announced sequentially and receive our diplomas.

This is an encouragement to every student out there to find the purpose in learning what you need to learn and shoot higher than you think you can go.

THE CESPEDES FAMILY

Giana

I continued taking college classes with my sisters. I spread out my general-education courses over time since some of these were pretty challenging for me. I had considered becoming a teacher at one point but the math was too hard for me. I tried getting my baking certificate but didn't have the motivation to finish.

I remember telling one of my classmates that I was feeling stressed over choosing my major and figuring out what I wanted to do with my life. He started cracking up, and said, "That's hilarious! You're only twelve years old!"

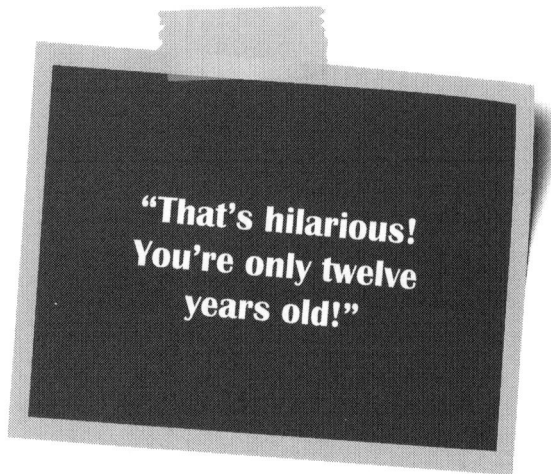

I know it may have seemed ridiculous for a twelve-year-old to be considering such big-picture life questions but it was true—I really was ready to pursue something fully and with my whole heart.

I realized I could do that with sign language. Sign Language 101 was the first class I took by myself. I was so excited about it, I came home jumping up and down. I fell in love with sign language during this class. I was a little intimidated by my teacher but confident that I could excel. After falling in love with sign language, I decided to take more and more sign classes.

When I started to really enjoy and appreciate my studies in American Sign Language, I found myself wishing that it was the only subject I was taking. I loved practicing. And, although I took a bunch of really interesting and enjoyable classes like culinary and baking courses, I couldn't wait to get back to my signing.

People told me that I was good at sign language and said that I had lots of potential. There was no question that I loved it. And, knowing that all the time and effort I put into it was sure to yield results, I believed that I could learn it well. I was really dedicated and wanted to become as good at it as possible.

I started Professor Deborah Sison's class when I was twelve years old and she has been with me throughout my entire college experience. She took me under her wing and nurtured my love and skill in sign language. Along the way, she became my second mom. She was my professor for most of my interpreting classes and is largely responsible for all that I have learned.

I owe a lot to Professor Sison and she has earned a special place in my heart. She took extra time to help me with the coursework as well as with understanding the importance of dedication. And, she held me to the same standards as everyone else, even though I was young. She knew that I was going to have to actively pursue deaf people, make friends in class, and open myself up to embracing a skill I would use for the rest of my life. So, she helped me break down whatever homeschool shell I had developed.

As I mentioned earlier, I graduated from COC with my Associates Degree (AA) in American Sign Language Interpreting at sixteen years of age, after four and a half years of college (winter, spring, summer and fall semesters). I was the youngest person to graduate in the entire school (about

2,200 people), with a solid 3.5 GPA. I received a medal at my graduation for my 3.8 GPA in the interpreting program. Through COC, I went to numerous events for the deaf.

Now, sign language is central in my life.

After traveling to Georgia post-graduation, to immerse myself in deaf culture, I was selected to go to the Registry for Interpreters for the Deaf (RID) interpreters' conference. I went to learn how to better become a professional, network with other professionals, and communicate with those in the deaf culture.

While there, I met CJ Jones, a deaf comedian/actor, well-known in the deaf community. (He acted in the movie *Baby Driver* and will act in the new *Avatar* movie coming out.) I got to volunteer for several of his events and have become good friends with him.

I have also met several other deaf celebrities, including, Robert DeMayo, T.L. Forsberg, Kristy Mahe (deaf model and actress), Jody Stevenson (deaf model and actress), Ryan Lane (actor in *Switched at Birth*), and the ladies who do the videos for DPAN.TV—The Sign Language Channel.

Taking a Gap Year

Giana

I am currently a freelance interpreter for Accurate Communications Agency and interpret at church every week. My ultimate goal is to be RID-NIC certified as an American Sign Language Interpreter and then find an interpreting specialty (medical or law) to pursue.

In the Fall of 2017, before starting my current job, I took a gap year and went to a one-year intensive GAP program

PRODUCTIVE HOMESCHOOLING

called Worldview at the Abbey in Canon City, Colorado. I was there to learn philosophy, politics, apologetics, economics and various other subjects through a Christian worldview.

Throughout the two semesters that comprised the GAP program, there were extensive reading and writing assignments. I was hoping that the year would help me improve my reading comprehension and writing abilities.

I struggled along—and then I discovered audiobooks. They made so much difference in my ability to learn, I often say that they saved my life. I had never thought of myself as an auditory learner until I found audiobooks. That's when I discovered that listening and following along works very well for me.

I could not have wished for a better year. Of course, there were intense rough patches but the friendships, the knowledge gained, and the community we built from nothing was quite a dream. During that year, I learned truth I did not even know was out there.

I always had light bulbs going off in class, as I learned things that dramatically expanded my world. My favorite part of the day was when we finished class and walked to lunch in groups, discussing topics covered in class. We became so enthusiastic about things we were learning, and so amazed, we often ended up shouting with joy on our way to lunch.

Every student was likeminded in the pursuit of truth and the knowledge of those things which are real and true. More than once, I passed my fellow students engrossed in conversation and overheard snippets of conversation like, "So, what do *you* think about predestination and free will?"

Inevitably, I would be unable to stop myself from joining in and maturely discussing with each person their beliefs and how they came to believe the way they did.

At the Abbey, we read various authors all the way from B.C through A.C., including, among others: Plato, Aristotle, Augustine, Pascal, Descartes, St. Athanasius, Langland,

THE CESPEDES FAMILY

G.K Chesterton, C.S. Lewis, Rousseau, Paine, Hobbes, Shakespeare, O'Conner, and so many other influential writers from every century. It was amazing to learn how much these philosophers' writings still influence our world today.

As I've developed a love of philosophy, it has given me a new lens through which I now see the world. I have childlike wonder for the small things, just like when G.K. Chesterton said in one of his many parables, "Ordinary things are more valuable than extraordinary things; nay, they are more extraordinary." The small things are more amazing than extraordinary things in life.

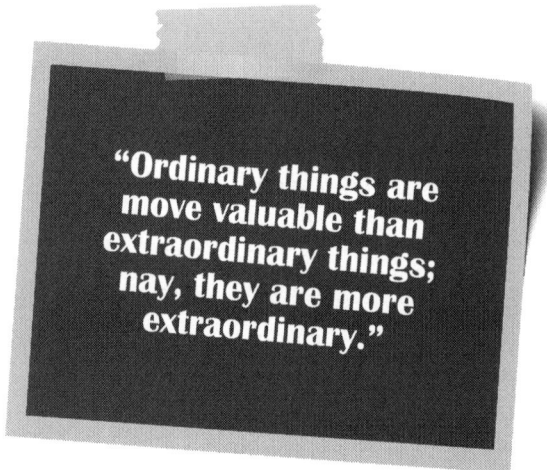

"Ordinary things are move valuable than extraordinary things; nay, they are more extraordinary."

Throughout my year in the GAP Program, I did not get to utilize my interpreting much. I did interpret weekly at a small Baptist church. I got hired to interpret for a student at CSU-Pueblo Colorado State but unfortunately, that did not work out.

Initially, I had been afraid to leave home and live independently in Colorado. I had never been separated from my family for longer than a couple of weeks. Ultimately, I

PRODUCTIVE HOMESCHOOLING

decided to take a huge leap of faith and live on my own. It was the best decision I ever made in my life.

I grew so much by taking that gap year, attending the GAP Program and living on my own. My character has also been enriched by trials I encountered at the Abbey and trials I knew were going on back at home, namely my papa's worsening cancer. I cannot wait to learn more and serve God as I have come to know and love Him.

HOMESCHOOLING BLESSINGS AND BENEFITS

Ivana

I really enjoyed my homeschooling years. In my earliest days, homeschooling was what I knew and all I knew. It gave us girls the luxury of devoted parenting, and the opportunity to fully respond to our schooling. Instead of being taught by a teacher provided by an away-from-home school, we had Mom and Dad as our teachers—the two people who knew and loved us best. Because our parents were our teachers, they knew how to tailor our education to match our strengths and weaknesses. So, we had the most effective education possible and were able to truly learn and grow.

I loved showing off how much I knew because I knew how happy it would make Mom. She invested her whole self into us and was there for us through everything. We felt like she was *ours*. It was such a blessing to never have to feel the lack of a mom in our lives. I had many friends who did not have that kind of accessibility to their parents.

As we got older, we felt a little bit of an absence created by Dad's need to be off earning a living so he could take care of us all. After all, he was the husband to Mom and the dad to us five girls. That was a lot of people to provide for and protect.

From as far back as I can remember, I valued the time, attention and guidance my parents gave me and my sisters. I was always so grateful for these blessings. I have never doubted the tremendous impact this has had on who I have become.

Mom was always correcting and guiding our thinking. She reminded us that we had more than we could have ever dreamed of having. She also reminded us that whatever we had was a gift from above, not something we had by our own right. That included what we got to eat, wear, do—everything. She made sure that we were very aware of our family heritage, and always remembered those relatives living in other countries who did not live with the abundance we had been given.

Dad, meanwhile, always reminded us girls to laugh at our challenges. He was the one who brought humor into the house. He managed to find humor in every situation, even those situations that didn't seem at all funny.

"It's important to find comic relief when difficult things happen," Dad would say. "The same thing that's challenging today can be a really funny story later on."

On a more serious note, he always helped us realize that every situation was for our good, and better than what it might appear at any given moment.

Belicia

We loved homeschooling for so many reasons. It was very enjoyable going to amusement parks on "homeschool day" where there were absolutely no lines, taking vacations and having sleepovers whenever we felt like it. We also enjoyed the time we had together and the freedom of our schedule.

THE CESPEDES FAMILY

If we wanted to finish our school day early so that we could have a cooking competition or try to build a treehouse, we absolutely had that choice.

Homeschooling always kept us busy and that was another reason we loved it. We never reached a point where we had nothing to do. It was good to always have something purposeful and beneficial to accomplish.

We even did school throughout the summertime. The way I see it, three months off of school really means four. After kids return to school from summer, teachers have to spend at least a month reviewing, to make sure everyone is on the same page. Then there are fall, winter and spring breaks to take into account. When it all adds up, kids really spend more like seven months in school, and five months—almost half the year!—away from it. By simply putting in a few hours most days throughout the summer break periods, we were able to learn the same material in almost half the time.

I understand that having school all year round might strike some of you as awful or extreme. We had too many friends, activities, events, and parties all the time to see ourselves as suffering. We were not workaholics (or study-aholics!) in any sense of the word.

Here was our typical school-week schedule: we went to school for twenty hours a week, total, usually spread out over the weekdays. We also had six hours of tennis, six hours of church activities, twenty hours with friends, at least one party, Knott's Berry Farm day, and three hours of garage-sale shopping. The rest of our time was devoted to playing.

We also did schoolwork during holidays, on vacations and even sometimes on the weekends. You see, for me (and I believe for my sisters as well), school was just another fun activity that involved learning and a little bit of brain exercise. I attribute my perspective on school to my mom. Not only did she pick our curriculum with that sense of fun, but she was always very balanced. She never got mad at us if we failed to grasp something. Not at all.

School was just another fun activity that involved learning and a little bit of brain exercise.

Instead, Mom would take that opportunity to gather everyone together and have the closest thing we had to a class time. That's where the whiteboard made its appearance, and Mom would explain the concept, ask questions, and have a small quiz at the end. Knowing that we girls were all at different points in our learning, Mom would simplify the questions and adapt them to each of us as need be. That was another major upside of homeschooling—the freedom to individualize a topic to match the student.

In typical schools, teachers have to handle thirty to forty kids at once. They have to instruct all of those unique brains at the same time. They have no choice but to teach to the least advanced level in the class. Teachers try to bring everyone to the same level, but the truth is, we are just not made that way. All of us are different, with different strengths and weaknesses, different ways of learning things, and varying subjects that we understand—or don't.

THE CESPEDES FAMILY

In homeschooling, we had a one-on-one teacher who knew us intimately, loved us deeply, cared about bringing out the best in us, and taught each of us our own personalized curriculum. We would read the book, do the problems, look at the examples, and ask Mom for explanations. We also had certain subjects and class times we would all do together at the same time.

I realize that this concept of homeschool learning may be new for some readers, so I will illustrate using geography—one of the subjects we would all do together. Papa was always our geography teacher. He would gather us around at a certain point of the day and show us a map. Then he would recite a few different facts and give us a small history lesson pertaining to the geographical area he was addressing that day.

He would direct some facts to us older girls, saying things like, "Europe was the central point of both World Wars. It is now united under the European Union, which allows all of the countries to combine their military forces and currency."

Then, he would say to Briana, the third youngest, "There are about fifty countries in Europe. Which one do you think is the biggest?"

Then he would point to the map, saying, "Yup! It's Russia. And what about the smallest? It's a tiny country called Vatican City. Ask your big sisters what the Vatican is all about."

Lastly, he would turn to Giana, the youngest at the time, saying, "See how big Europe is? Well, it is actually the second-smallest continent! But that doesn't stop it from being home to many, many people. Eight hundred million people live there. Can you imagine eight hundred million people?" This lesson from Papa is one great example of why we girls loved homeschooling.

I'm sure you can see how the pattern of our family lifestyle and the flexibility of our schedule contributed to our love for homeschooling. Another huge factor was the oppor-

PRODUCTIVE HOMESCHOOLING

tunity for acceleration. There came a point in our schooling when we realized, "Hey, what if we got up a little earlier, and did our school work for tomorrow? Then we'd have a whole day freed up!"

Well, that work for tomorrow turned into our work for next week, next month, and even next year. We were passing grades so quickly, we all became motivated to get to the next one. Besides, Mama would take us out for ice cream every time we "graduated" to the next grade.

Funny enough, this desire for acceleration started all the way back when I was a first-grader. I loved my big sister Nana so much. (Yep, that's Ivana's nickname, pronounced Naana with a long 'a' instead of like the nickname for Grandma.) All I wanted in the whole world was to be just like her, so naturally I wanted to catch up with her and be in the same grade.

Mama gave me the final exam early. When I passed, I was able to go right into second grade with my big sis. She wasn't too thrilled about it then, but she eventually got used to it. She wasn't too thrilled about me graduating college before her either, but I know she's proud of me.

HOMESCHOOLING CHALLENGES AND PITFALLS

Briana

As the middle child, I have an interesting place in the family. Growing up, I certainly felt like I fit in, but in my own unique way. The fact that each of us girls felt so different than the others now strikes me as funny. I think that the diversity within our family is what makes us so unique.

I've always been the one that loved nature. The outdoors was my best friend. I preferred to go outside and pretend to be a Native American camping by our backyard tree than to sit inside and do algebra. My love of the outdoors also went along with a love of getting dirty and physically working as hard as I could.

When I was young and in elementary grades, I loved being homeschooled. I loved the flexibility of my schedule, the joy of being around my sisters, the ability to play outside or take vacations and do school at the same time.

PRODUCTIVE HOMESCHOOLING

Elementary homeschooling was great but, as I grew, I craved a public-school type of experience. One of my favorite memories of homeschool involved a similar structure and I really enjoyed it. Ivana and Belicia were teaching Giana and me classes like anatomy, character training and reading comprehension. Every morning, we would gather in the playroom, sit on our beanbags with notebooks in hand and be taught like we were in a classroom, complete with a whiteboard and all.

Those classes taught by my sisters gave me a purpose for getting up in the morning, and the feeling that I was going to *school*. I was being graded, watched and guided, and I loved it. (Also, because Giana and I were the only ones being taught, I could tell myself I was the best student in class.) I thrived within that kind of structure and still remember some of the things I learned from those classes.

When we girls got to high school grades, Mom didn't teach us through the courses but let all of us do independent learning. The independent study method worked well for my sisters but I felt like I needed something different. In chemistry, for example, I had a tutor. I loved having a guide—someone to explain a difficult concept to me by using their personal stories and giving me examples. I find that concepts make much more sense to me and are much easier for me to internalize when people tell me stories or offer real-life application.

For high school, I would have preferred the structure of the classroom and a teacher to guide me. This was my personal preference. Psychology was my first high school course and I approached it with great excitement. I envisioned being able to take it really slowly. I wanted to read every word, and go over all the textbook material several times, including the introduction and table of contents. I wanted to enjoy learning the material at my own pace.

Watching my sisters quickly accelerate through their coursework, I overrode my natural inclination to go slowly and really absorb the material. Instead, I put pressure on myself to keep up with the pace of my sisters. I switched my focus to keeping up with the compelling speed of my family, and finishing the course. Being out of step with my sisters' pace of learning made me feel left behind.

On the one hand, homeschool high school gave me a lot of independence. On the other hand, by rushing to keep up with my sisters, I became more dependent upon Mom as a minute-by-minute tutor because I needed guidance.

I always wanted to be one of the big girls. Thanks to my desire to be at the same level as my big sisters, I didn't stop to think that it might be unrealistic for me and my style of learning. And of course, I was encouraged by others, thanks to my intense drive to get my schoolwork done. What parent wouldn't want to see that kind of drive in one of their children?

Encouragement is typically a wonderful thing to offer your children but, in my case, it only fueled my drive to go at a speed faster than would have been natural for me.

The same was true of my mom's excellent planning. "Bri," she would say, "if you finish by this deadline, we can apply to this college and get in your first semester here."

Thus, I was motivated to go *even faster* than my older sisters, not stopping to think that I probably should have taken another year for high school. Instead, I felt an internal pressure to rush through.

Overall, high school ended up being something to get through—a checklist rather than a time to learn material that I would use in my life. The high school years were a crucial time for me and, given my love of structure, I think a classroom setting would have satisfied my educational needs and left me better prepared.

Sometimes I ask myself, *What would the impact on my life have been if I had gone to a high school classroom with other students my age?*

PRODUCTIVE HOMESCHOOLING

I also wonder, *What about all the negative stereotypes applied to high school students? Would I have adopted those characteristics if I were around that attitude eight hours a day?*

I am also aware of the reality that public school is geared toward the lowest common denominator, which means that the averages will be adjusted to that speed. I don't like that aspect of public school or the fact that all students are forced to decelerate their learning in order to match the learning speed of the slowest learners in class. There is so much time wasted reviewing material at a classroom level.

It is one thing for me to review material as I need to in order to get my work done—but that's different than being *required* to repeatedly review material I have already learned. I know that in a sixteen-week semester, I would have been capable of accomplishing at least twice as much as what is expected in classrooms today. (Adults don't always give teenagers credit for their actual capabilities, often lumping everyone in with the worst of the lot.)

I recognize that there were many advantages to the way I did school. I can also say with full confidence that homeschooling is a beautiful method of education because it allows the parents to:

- give their students the opportunity to focus on themselves;
- provide for the student's individual needs;
- highlight the student's strengths and weaknesses so they can be the best student possible; and
- invest in their children's lives in the most personal way possible.

To all you parents out there, I would encourage you to listen to your child. If they are more like me, consider putting them in school with a classroom, classmates, and a teacher—

even if it means they won't accelerate as much. I believe parents have to decide what they think is truly important for their kid, and what they will emphasize in their schooling.

Ask yourselves, *What's most important to us? Good grades? Mastery? Acceleration? Simply having our children enjoy learning?*

I am sharing my story with you readers so that you will see the real side of our family. We did nothing perfectly but everything excellently. Everything done for our education had a purpose, an intention that was much more than just getting good grades. There are many ways that a child can be homeschooled. The method used by my family is one of many.

Dyslexia

Giana

Growing up, I always felt different than the rest of my sisters. For starters, I took longer to start reading than they did, so I

PRODUCTIVE HOMESCHOOLING

didn't start elementary homeschooling until I was six—a little bit late in my family. Once I did start school, it took more time for me to learn things, which made me feel slower intellectually.

In one of my earliest memories of my education, I was with Mom as she bought our elementary curriculum. We did basic grammar, reading comprehension, arithmetic and English. Mom had been teaching us some educational basics like the alphabet, phonics, tracing and simple arithmetic since we were infants.

During my homeschool time with Mom, we would sit down and take one subject at a time. Every day was different but reading and writing was my primary focus. I had a lot of trouble with reading, writing and spelling so I never felt like I was smart. I've always been an auditory learner rather than a reading-and-writing learner and it was hard to glean the content contained in books. I needed consistency and I needed time.

We worked through the books with flexibility, depending on what I could handle. When we got to a subject that I could do alone like science or math, Mom would let me study alone so I could build some independent skill.

Homeschooling was a big challenge for me in certain ways, considering that the cornerstone of this method of schooling is based on reading and writing. Mom was there to guide me and provide me with examples, but she wasn't *teaching* me the material, per sé. I had to rely on my ability to learn from the books, and that was really hard for me and has remained so throughout my life.

Nana (Ivana) and Lily (Belicia) started reading at three years old but I was still struggling with phonics at eight years old. I took almost twice as long as my sisters to learn the same materials and develop the same skills. You can imagine how discouraging this was for me as a little kid. I was trying really hard, but I got frustrated and antsy. I thought something was really wrong with me because *I just didn't get it.*

THE CESPEDES FAMILY

At one point, Mom started compensating because she saw that something was off with me. To test my audio perception, she would read to me the chapter and ask me questions. I was able to answer all the questions. Then, she handed me the book for my turn to read and I seemed to become mentally exhausted within minutes. It took me fifteen minutes to get through a small paragraph and a few hours to get through a chapter.

I didn't like that time of day, having to go so painstakingly through my reading, but Mom understood and helped me push through. Sometimes she spent so much time with me, my sisters would say, "Mom, can it be our turn with you now?"

By the end of the school day, I was mentally exhausted. I was more than ready to go outside and play and swim, or stay inside and play with stuffed animals and dolls. I always had a really good imagination. I had over twenty different stuffed animals, and I gave them all names, ages and stories. I also spent hours playing with my Polly Pockets dolls, making up stories for them as I played.

Before Mom took me to get professionally tested and I got diagnosed with dyslexia and dysgraphia, I labored for so long, trying to understand my learning difficulties. I felt dumb even when I had a lot of extra help. The constant comparison to my older sisters didn't help either. I would feel humiliated when I was trying to do simple tasks, like reading aloud in front of people or coming up with creative answers that demonstrated my comprehension of a topic. I still struggle with this, even though it's improved a lot over the years.

I cannot even imagine what would have happened to me had I been in the public-school system with my learning difficulties. Dyslexia is not typically tested for, despite the fact that it is estimated that one out of every five people are born with it. So, based on my learning difficulties, my teachers probably would have thought that I was a bad student, or had Attention Deficient Hyperactivity Disorder, and given me medication to "fix" me. I would have been labeled, marginalized, and maybe even bullied because I wasn't as smart as the other kids.

Mom never gave up on me. She spent hours each day reading and reading to me, even with the responsibility of the home and three other school-age daughters to attend to. I am so grateful for her faithfulness in my life. I know I wouldn't be where I am today without her by my side every day.

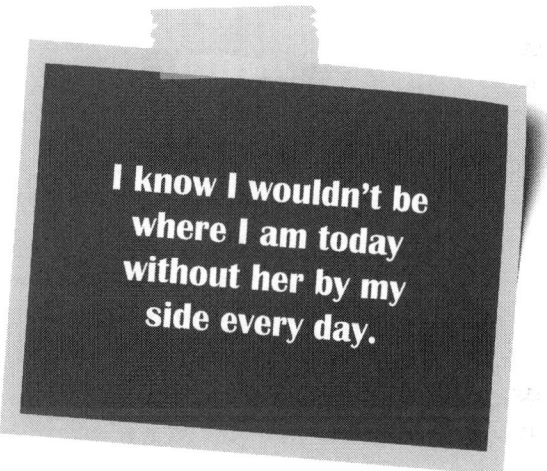

I heartily recommend that when parents or teachers notice in their children/students struggles similar to mine, they commit to getting to the bottom of the trouble in a kind and gentle way. Communicate with the kid so you can get them the help they need and get a diagnosis. It's hard to find solutions to a problem that has not been identified.

To all of you kids out there with any form of mental or physical challenge, I want to encourage you. I have personally seen myself grow and learn from my experiences and it has made me a more disciplined individual than I would have been had it been easy. Yes, I have to work harder than other people to understand, but I have learned that failure and success are equally important in life. And as I live my life, I learn to appreciate the struggle.

Four Grades in One Year

Giana

As I've explained, elementary school was rough. But I wanted to catch up to my sisters, so I would go longer than I had to in school.

"You're determined to be the same age as the grade you're in, aren't you?" said Mom. She was right.

After completing my elementary schooling, I took the CAT exam to test out of my junior high grades. I tested above average in math, and average in every other subject. Therefore, my grade caught up to my age and I was a nine-year-old in ninth grade. This put me directly into high school.

I went through the same high school as my sisters did—the American School of Correspondence, but took the general-education path rather than the college preparatory path. (We used all the curriculum of this special-function, accredited high school. By going through this high school curriculum in homeschool, we were able to proceed at our own pace.)

On July 5th, 2011 as I turned eleven years old, I began a dedicated ten-month journey through high school with the goal of beating my sisters to the high-school finish line.

PRODUCTIVE HOMESCHOOLING

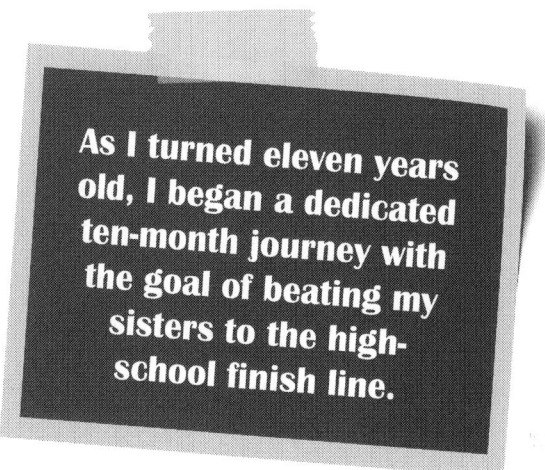

As I turned eleven years old, I began a dedicated ten-month journey with the goal of beating my sisters to the high-school finish line.

Mama Vicki

Once Giana was diagnosed with dyslexia, it helped us to understand what was going on and why. It also helped us to know what accommodations we could make to assist her learning and her success. She knew she would have to work harder than her sisters. She also realized that she was not ignorant and if she applied herself, she would be able to accomplish whatever she set her mind to. And that's exactly what she did. The diagnosis gave us great clarity and was a huge turning point for Giana. It gave her the motivation to keep striving.

Giana

I said to myself, *Just get through high school! You can learn in college.*
    That might not have been the greatest motto, but I had already heard from so many of my public-school friends that they hated their high school years. I felt weary just listening to them talk about all the drama they experienced.

Then there were my dad's stories. "In high school, I would unknowingly break girls' hearts because I didn't realize they were in love with me. Then the next thing I knew, their brothers would come and pick a fight with me for no reason!"

I was glad that the path I had chosen to follow in high school enabled me to avoid all the drama.

I did one subject at a time. I began with psychology—and finished in three days. I was really motivated to catch up to my sisters. Once I finished a course, I would go on to the next one.

The hardest part was learning to study independently of Mom. I was forced to learn from the books themselves, although I could always go to my mom with questions. I relied on her quite a bit because the material was hard for me. She helped me understand the assignment by presenting the question in a real-life context or re-explaining it in simpler terms. From there, I was able to finish the rest of the assignment on my own.

I was fueled by my determination to be in the same grade as my age. Knowing I had started high school when I was eleven, I wanted to make sure I finished eleventh grade before I turned twelve.

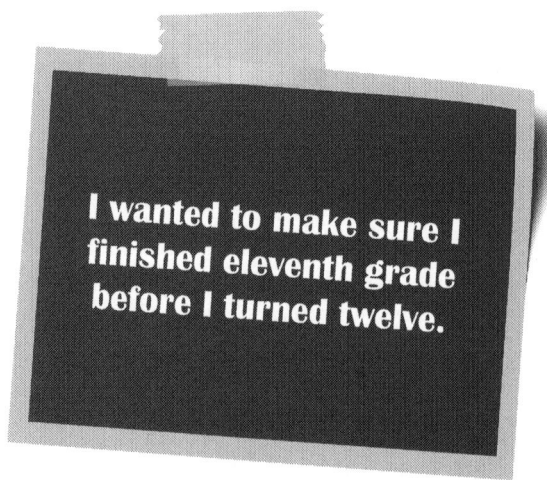

All the girls were already in college and I felt a lot of pressure to keep on par with them. I found it especially challenging when people would say, "All your sisters are in college and excelling. Are you going to graduate as early as them?" Or, "Is your GPA as high as theirs? Have you actually learned anything because you're doing school so fast?"

I spent extra hours studying every day and graduated high school in the same year that I began it. I was really proud of myself. Graduating at eleven years of age was a huge success for me.

I would joke, "None of my sisters graduated younger than age thirteen, so you could say they are underachievers!"

It was so satisfying to know that I had pushed through the challenges and complications that went along with having dyslexia. I didn't let it keep me from reaching my goals.

Anorexia

Briana

I want to share a very interesting season in my life. When I was twelve years old, I started to become hyperaware of the amount of food I was eating each day. I felt like I was doing something wrong in the way I was eating.

I started to control my food intake, and that control quickly turned into an obsession. In my desire to be in control, I became compulsive about planning every calorie. I was overly aware of every part of my body and, because all my attention was centered on myself, I was miserable.

For the next two years, my life shrunk. I was focused only on my next meal and getting my high school exams done. I was determined to avoid being fat at all costs, and

THE CESPEDES FAMILY

to burn every calorie I consumed. As a result, I got deathly skinny. I reached a point where I could put my hands under my ribs and touch the other side of them.

My mom recognized what was happening and came alongside me lovingly. She strongly urged me to recognize the lies that were consuming my thoughts and heart and replace them with God and His truth—my only hope for overcoming this vicious cycle. I knew that she was praying for me earnestly.

Nevertheless, I became enveloped in myself and in food, completely self-centered and insular. I was living in a prison, caged in a place inside myself I couldn't seem to escape.

This could be called anorexia.

The point I am trying to make here is this: I could have experienced the same thing in public school. Regardless of what kind of school you go to, or what kind of family you come from, you can still experience issues like depression, anorexia and bulimia. These challenges can befall anyone. They are a matter of what is going on in the mind and heart and can occur independent of your particular circumstances.

In my case, my circumstances were great. I brought *myself* into captivity. I didn't need public school to have body issues.

When I was thirteen years old, I went to Honduras to help with missions, spend several months amongst the locals, and learn Spanish. Being alone in a third-world country, I learned a lot about myself and about God. I discovered who I was and became aware of the prison in which I had unknowingly jailed myself.

In Honduras, I experienced a moment of surrender. I said, "God, take the key to my heart. Please grab it from me. I'm tired of being in control."

It was in that same spirit that I received news recently that I passed what was to me un-passable: the California First Year Law Student's Examination. I had told my dad that I would do it, even though I had no motivation to do so.

This was my third attempt at taking the exam, and after the first two attempts, I really did not want to continue doing law school. But because I had promised my Dad, I spent countless long hours of studying over eighteen months. I endured and finished, without any expectation of passing.

God blessed that work, and I successfully passed the Baby Bar! Unbelievable. This was one of the biggest hurdles I have ever gotten over. Passing this exam has given me many opportunities.

I have learned so much from being homeschooled. I wouldn't change my path, for I know that the Lord used it for the best. I am so excited to see what will happen in the future. The biggest lesson I've learned overall is to turn over control to God and enjoy that process. My advice to others is to enjoy being a kid when you're a kid and being an adult when you're an adult.

Overcoming Obstacles

Ivana

Some of my earliest memories of Dad involved him teaching us Proverbs from the Bible, and coming home after his first surgery for papillary thyroid cancer (which has since spread to his lungs). I was only seven years old at the time. Dad vomited and experienced terrible pain for several weeks straight, with Mom right by his side.

I've always known my dad as a sick man, but strong and athletic. Because of his strength and athleticism, people didn't realize he was so sick. It was always tricky navigating those waters, and especially difficult when I got into my pre-teen and teen years.

THE CESPEDES FAMILY

We butted heads on a lot of issues. The truth was, my dad was a feisty Latino and as his daughter, I was the female version of him. We were both decisive leaders with strong opinions, and hard-headed, go-getter types. So, we were bound to collide on certain things.

When I was in my preteens and early teen years, I struggled with my weight and my self-image. I was very self-conscious of my body and very insecure. At the same time, I was pondering all the usual life questions that go along with being a teenager—only, I was no ordinary teenager. I was a fourteen-year-old high school graduate.

Graduating at only fourteen years old, I had major fear over what came next. I was five or six years ahead of my peers and subjected to unkind scrutiny and criticism from them. People get funny when you are so young when you graduate high school—a little bit jealous and judgmental.

We girls were raised with a conservative lifestyle and that included our dress and speech code. The fact that I was finished with school by eleven in the morning and got to have playtime seven days a week while other students were at school didn't help everyone's jealousy issues either.

"Graduating at fourteen years old? That's not right!" People didn't understand us because our experience as homeschooled students was so different than theirs. We were constantly dealing with the misconceptions and judgments of others. To be dealing with it when I was only a teenager was very challenging.

I was also a tennis player in a family of competitive tennis players and Dad was my tennis coach. When he was in his coaching role, he was tough on me. He was always pushing me to excel and be my best. The thing is, I already had so much on my plate, I needed him more as a dad than as a coach. I didn't respond well to the change in our relationship dynamic from father-daughter to coach-player.

I often went home from tennis practice in tears, crying to my mom, saying, "Mom, I'm dealing with my body and Dad and I don't know what to do! I don't want a coach! I want a dad." On top of the anguish I was already feeling, I felt guilty for having those feelings about my sick dad. I had been dealing heavily with his cancer my whole life.

Ultimately, the struggles I experienced with my dad became the firm foundation for lessons I would carry with me through the next stages of my life. For an entire year, Mom sat down with me for an hour at a time every evening. She guided and loved me, reminding me of the Biblical truth.

"When your dad and I first met," she told me, "I really struggled for that whole first year. We weren't yet believers and I didn't know how to deal with the thoughts and feelings I was having. When your dad was late for dinner, for example, I would think he didn't care."

After Mom and Dad came to know Jesus, Mom adopted a unique practice to deal with her negative thoughts. She started what she called a thought journal. She would go into her prayer closet and write in her journal every thought that was negative, deceptive or just not God-honoring. After she wrote down all that nastiness, she went to the Scriptures.

As she was developing what she called her "treadmill of truth", she was training her mind. She practiced the truth over and over again in her head, like a spiritual ninja. This practice brought about an unbelievable change in Mom's life—and later in mine.

Mom became a student of the Word and a student of her own faith, and she taught me to be that way, as well. She had me write down my thoughts and then look for the pattern. I learned to recognize when I was thinking a lie over and over again.

"Look at the promises God has made to you," she would say. "If you choose to believe a lie, it's not the lie's fault and it's not Dad's fault. See what I mean?"

She helped me realize that it was *my own* fault if I continually chose to believe the same lie. She taught me to choose to believe in the truth of the Scriptures and God's promises. I do this by writing down the lie and then, beside it, writing God's Scriptures and promises. In that way, I can combat any lie with the Truth with a capital T.

It turns out that the keys to the kingdom spoken of in the Bible are actually the keys to mental, spiritual and emotional freedom. The Truth frees you from your own faulty thinking. I can't think of a more important or practical lesson.

HOMESCHOOLING IS NOT FOR EVERYONE

Mama Vicki

It is clear to me that homeschooling was definitely God's best for our family—but that doesn't mean that I think it is best for *all* families. Every family has different needs.

Each of our daughters experienced her upbringing in her own unique way. And, I'm aware that when it comes time to make decisions about educating their own children (if they are blessed with them), my daughters may choose to go another route. That is fine with me. All that matters to me is what God wants for them.

I also believe that time sweetens all memories and that my girls will discover even deeper and sweeter memories of their homeschooling years as time goes by. They are already so charitable and gracious about this time of their lives.

I know that I too will continue to discover even greater depth and sweetness as time passes and I reflect back and contemplate this time of our lives. I had the privilege of teaching our daughters how to read and sharing with them my own persistent hunger for learning. I got to study their hearts, discover the unique ways God had created them, and encourage and support them as they expressed and pursued these leanings. I got to make decisions related to the content that I did and did not want entering their young hearts and minds. For starters, I guided them to the Word of God, the works of great thinkers, and books about wholesome topics, written in wholesome language.

Since we were together most of the time, I also got to witness their physical, emotional, spiritual, and relational development. Having had a front-row seat in their lives at that time is a priceless gift that I hold dear to my heart. The girls also had front-row seats in each other's lives, as well, and I believe that they too cherish that gift. It has given them deeper relationships, the fullness of which they will continue to discover as they mature.

Now, as adults, they may or may not consider each other best friends as some move away and other likeminded ladies with similar interests become part of their lives. I do trust that all of our girls will remain close, cherished, lifetime friends. I believe this not just because they are blood sisters, but because they have closely shared the foundational part of their upbringing. This too is a gift that was given to each of them, and one I hope they will appreciate more and more as they mature.

Tailoring Your Child's Education

For Jan and I, the decision to homeschool had already been made. We based our decision on several factors, including:

PRODUCTIVE HOMESCHOOLING

- ☞ A commitment to value-centered education;
- ☞ Our strong and undeniable conviction for Christian discipleship;
- ☞ The desire to have the privilege of investing in the little hearts and minds of our young daughters;
- ☞ The need to instill in our daughters the values we believed to be most important;
- ☞ The desire to keep a watchful eye on our daughters' leanings, strengths and passions; and
- ☞ The need to know how to best tailor the ministry to their hearts.

Deciding whether or not to homeschool was one thing. Now we had to figure out how to tailor our girls' education according to everything I've listed above. Assessing the direction for the road ahead was the tricky part. It was an art, really.

We were starting from the unknown and seeking direction. I spent a lot of time on my knees, feeling blind, praying for wisdom, guidance and direction. I was now tasked with educating our girls, and doing so on very limited finances.

After much prayer and thought, I realized that there was only one place to start: with the girls' hearts. Before I could turn them into little students and achievers, I myself had to become a student of their hearts. There was no way forward except to move forward, trying many, many new things, watching my daughters' reactions to things, as well as their leanings and delights. And, all the while, staying connected to them. That was going to be key.

We tried everything and anything, including, just to name a few:

- ☞ playing sports like tennis and swimming;
- ☞ pursuing music, like studying the piano or going to a concert; and

THE CESPEDES FAMILY

☞ introducing business concepts via business outings, such as a visit to Jan's office, a lawyer's office, a senior home and a doctor's office.

We introduced the girls to many different types of people, environments, skills and knowledge. We took them to Mexico to visit my family and to Honduras to encourage opportunities to serve, while at the same time opening up the girls' hearts and minds to things like the global world God made, the way others live, the noble characters found in humble settings, the reality of poverty and suffering, and the profound beauty of simplicity. Wherever we went and whatever we were doing, I kept an eye on where their little hearts lit up.

Your family will find your own path and your own learning adventures as you go. And when you're questioning your readiness to meet the challenges of guiding your little student, remember that no one can tailor your child's education better than you, their parent(s).

If you decide to homeschool, you get to choose the values you want to instill in your child, rather than leaving that to the public schools. In homeschooling, you have the opportunity to be more intentional and purposeful in that quest. And take it from me—it is quite an amazing privilege to gain access to the heart of your child.

Jan and I have always viewed our children as precious gifts from God, given to us for just a short time. By tailoring our children's educations to their hearts' desires, leanings, interests and passions, we ended up with students who couldn't wait to get out of bed in the morning to start their day. As a result, homeschooling became a vehicle of productivity beyond our wildest dreams.

PRODUCTIVE HOMESCHOOLING

Homeschooling became a vehicle of productivity beyond our wildest dreams.

TRANSITIONING FROM SCHOOL TO WORK

Belicia

In July of 2013, I graduated with my Bachelor of Science in Business Administration (BSBA) in Accounting/CPA. That was the first time I had *no* school whatsoever. For the next four months, from August to December, I had the busiest break time of my life. It was so weird for me to wake up and have no assignments to submit, spreadsheets to edit, papers to write, or books to read.

For the first time, I wasn't even allowed to study. I was practically commanded by my mom to relax. I can remember sitting down for a movie night without my computer or notebook on my lap, and my sisters asking, "Wait, Lily's not doing anything while we watch a movie?!"

Then they would turn to me with a look of shock, saying, "You're just going to sit down and watch?"

PRODUCTIVE HOMESCHOOLING

It did feel strange to me to just sit and watch a movie. I was so used to posting discussions or reviewing my notes with one eye while watching Batman run through the streets of Gotham with the other.

That being said, I still never allowed myself to truly have nothing to do. I kept myself plenty busy but, for the first time, I was busy with things other than academics. I had the opportunity to meet friends for lunch, have sleepovers, cook more often, go play tennis any time, get involved in the audio ministry at church, and actually finish my cleaning chores. I enjoyed many privileges that had been set aside for the previous six months.

We even took a three-week long trip to Europe within those four months. My mom, my three sisters and I flew to Spain, and then took a cruise to France, Monaco, and Italy. At that time, we were celebrating my college graduation, as well as my older sister's anticipated graduation in October. (Yes, I did end up graduating before her.) She was seventeen years old, and was earning her Bachelor's in Liberal Arts with an emphasis in Natural Sciences from Thomas Edison College. We also celebrated the high school graduations of Briana who was thirteen and Giana who was eleven. As you can see, our academic achievements had a ripple effect, impacting our younger sisters and driving them to greater motivation at an earlier age.

For the remainder of 2013, our European trip, the holiday season, tennis, parties, friends, my involvement in the church, and countless other items kept me pretty distracted. Even so, my mind was constantly returning to the next step.

In November of 2013, a month after returning from the trip, I decided to walk into a practice CPA exam to test the waters and really see what the exam was all about.

THE CESPEDES FAMILY

Test Prep Tips

I chose to take Financial Accounting and Reporting (FAR) exam, as it was apparently the hardest one. Because of all I had read and heard about this exam (dubbed "Fear, Anxiety, and Remorse" as a spoof on the FAR acronym), I was a bit intimidated, to say the least.

Thanks to my mindset of experience rather than expectation to pass, however, I wasn't nervous at all. I knew that taking the exam would give me the surest way to prepare, study, attempt, and pass when it counted. While waiting for my results, I began studying to retake FAR. I did not expect that I would pass, as I was taking it as a practice exam so I would better know what to expect when I took it again.

The study program I chose to use is called CPAExcel. It is created by Wiley and provides video lectures, lesson text, practice questions, graded questions, and task-based simulations. This variety of study methods allowed me to go into as much depth as needed, without having to turn to other sources. I really appreciated having the extensive material broken down into small, bite-sized lessons. Every time I finished one, I knew I was making progress, even if my progress amounted to little more than spooning away at the mound of dirt.

Many people have asked me how I studied for the exams, especially due to their massive load of complex information. "How do you stay motivated to study the same things, eight to twelve hours a day"? Excellent question. Here are a few things that helped me:

- ✓ Pick a good study program. Everyone learns differently, so make sure that program is tailored to you; and remember, the goal is to be finished, not perfect.

I realized that every time I finished covering all the lessons, even if I hadn't gone as in-depth as I would have liked, I passed the section. Accountants are often stereotyped as perfectionists. Now, some are more extreme than others, but I think we can all agree that this is true to an extent.

I would never call myself a "Type A" person, but I still arrange my M&Ms by color, have a sequence to brushing my teeth, and always have to clear the little red notifications on my iPhone. You must let go of doing every single task on the to-do lists. You simply will not have time to watch every video, read every chapter, review every flashcard, take every practice question, and score 100% on every simulation.

Once I focused on actually *finishing* the material rather than *perfecting it*, only taking extra time on things I needed help understanding, I was actually able to finish and retain more information.

- ✓ Have short-short-term goals.

When I say short-term goals, I mean double-short-term. Especially towards those last days, I needed almost an hour-by-hour goal in order to stay motivated. For example, I would decide to finish three lessons before I took a lunch break, or get through a whole topic before I went to bed.

- ✓ Reward yourself when you accomplish these goals.

I always did this with either food or exercise (two of my very favorite things, even though that may seem contradictory). Diving into a bag of chips or going out for a run was always a sure way I could keep myself motivated and excited to actually finish anything. Don't let a test—or any other prerequisite to entry into something you love—prevent you from pursuing your dreams.

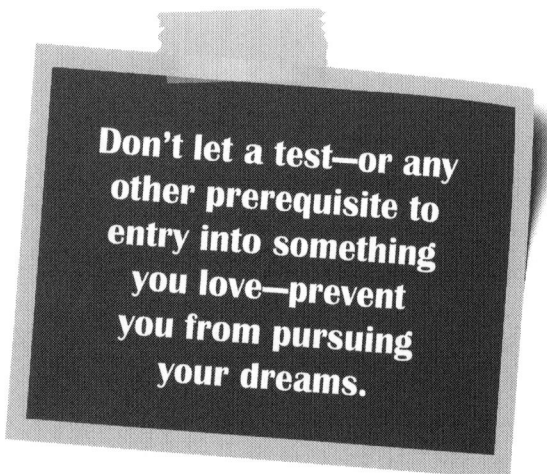

Go for it! We can't get too serious! Maybe it's just because I'm a teenager, but it's easier to run the marathon when I'm on a scooter.

✓   Have a positive support network around you.

I can't express how thankful I am to all the people who came alongside me to encourage me, pray for me, and check in with me constantly. Every time I had another exam scheduled, my mom would send out an update email, and I would receive a flood of notes. Many of these would come to mind in those moments where I needed the push, and the support really grew the whole process into a great life experience. It was awesome to be the tour guide, so to speak, in a huge adventure with some of my closest friends and relatives.

PRODUCTIVE HOMESCHOOLING

✓ Have a mindset of experience rather than expectation.

This is especially essential when actually taking the test, but also applies to the study process. Look at this time as preparation for your lifelong career. This really helped me, especially when I failed two sections of the exam (FAR and REG). My mom helped me to realize that I will be doing this for the rest of my life, so I might as well spend as much time as possible studying it.

This mindset also helped me pass the second time around. If you go into the exam with a mindset to learn from it, then you will know which subjects to target if you fall short your first time. Really what I'm trying to say is just *be thankful for how far you've come*! To have the opportunity to take this exam is a great and rare opportunity. Don't see it as a burden, or it will become one.

Let's not be those people who "know the price of everything and the value of nothing" (Oscar Wilde). Read and feed on this lovely quote below:

> "Be thankful that you don't already have everything you desire; if you did, what would there be to look forward to? Be thankful when you don't know something, for it gives you the opportunity to learn. Be thankful for the difficult times; during those times you grow. Be thankful for your limitations, because they give you opportunities for improvement. Be thankful for each new challenge, because it will build your strength and character. Be thankful for your mistakes, they will teach you valuable lessons. Be thankful when you're tired and weary, because it

THE CESPEDES FAMILY

means you've made a difference. It is easy to be thankful for the good things. A life of rich fulfillment comes to those who are also thankful for the setbacks. Gratitude can turn a negative into a positive. Find a way to be thankful for your troubles, and they can become your blessings."

~ Author Unknown

    The second time taking FAR (in January of 2014), I had not finished the study material, and so I felt pretty unequipped to retake the exam. My lack of preparation showed a few weeks later when I received a failing score.

    During that same testing window, I decided to take the Auditing (AUD) exam. This time around, I made it a point to finish the whole CPAExcel program for that exam. While having to wait for my results, I prepared to take FAR in the beginning of April, Business and Economic Concepts (BEC) in late April, and Regulation (REG) in May. This two-month window was by far the most intense testing time I had in my whole experience.

    Thankfully, I passed AUD, FAR, and BEC. After failing the FAR exam in January, I realized that I was taking too much time going through every single lesson, watching every video, studying every PowerPoint slide, reading every word of study text, answering every quiz question, and retaking every graded exam until I got 100%. Every time I finished all of the material, only doing the extra things on subjects I really struggled with, I would pass the exam. Unfortunately, I was not able to finish everything by the time I took REG. This was the only exam I hadn't had any college courses on, and so the material was all new to me.

    On August 19th, 2014, I was sitting in our leather reclining chair in the family room, half watching the Food

PRODUCTIVE HOMESCHOOLING

Network program *Chopped*, and feeling quite sick. The smell of lunch was starting to fill the air, and I was looking forward to taking a few bites and then crashing for a good nap. The day before, I had checked my scores for the REG exam that I had re-attempted on July 9th. I wasn't expecting the results to be published until after the weekend, which was another couple of days away.

The website read: AUD- PASS, BEC- PASS, FAR- PASS. For REG, it read: NO CREDIT. I was not expecting to pass, especially because I had previously taken it, and felt that I did about the same the second time around.

Ivana walked into the family room with a peaceful grin and mentioned that a couple of our friends had invited us out for lunch. I really wanted to take a raincheck for when I felt a bit more up to par, but we ended up meeting them at Rubio's just fifteen to twenty minutes later. Ivana asked me if I wanted to look a little nicer, and "paint the barn" (put on some makeup), but at the time, I honestly didn't care. I should have noticed the whispers and smirks going around the room amongst my sisters and my mom but my headache must have been clouding my judgment.

After a weird run-in with the cashier, three fish tacos, and a bunch of good laughs, we started heading back home. Our friends decided to come along and hang out for a few hours at the house, but I was honestly still looking forward to that nap. About five minutes from home, Ivana called Mama asking if we should pick up some pizza.

That was the first code word I actually picked up on.

"Pick up pizza?" I asked, "But we just ate!"

Ivana brushed it off and managed to contain her excitement. That is, until we pulled into our long driveway and saw about forty people come running out with signs and applause.

Absolutely *nothing* was registering. (Chalk it up to me feeling sick.) I began joining in the applause and congratu-

THE CESPEDES FAMILY

lating the girls in the car. "Good job! I don't know what you did, or which of you did it, but congrats!"

It wasn't until I saw a sign that read, "C.P.A- Constant Prayer Availeth," that I realized these people were here for *me*! I stepped out of the car and Dad handed me a print out. It read, "REG- 85 PASS." I could not believe it. (The AICPA posts No Credit when an exam has not yet been passed, and changes that status to Pass once the test-taker passes and their score is input. In my case, the input was delayed so I thought I had not passed. Later that same day, my Mom went online and discovered that the No Credit had been updated to Pass. She kept it to herself for the moment because she had surprise plans for me.)

I jumped into my dad's arms, then into my mom's in amazement. I cannot describe what it felt like to know that I was *done*. I had passed the CPA exam. No more fourteen-hour study days or mentally exhausting exams to earn this license.

So many of the people who were supporting me and praying for me came to celebrate with us, on literally an hour's notice. I made sure to take the time to thank each of them. After I hugged everyone, gave an impromptu speech, and made a few special dedications, a few of our friends lifted me up on their shoulders and took me for a victory lap around the crowd. I'll never forget that day. After partying for another several hours, I finally got that much needed sleep.

After passing the exam in July, I got my hours signed off by Mr. Bonenfant, took the ethics exam, and submitted my fingerprints and final documentation. I again have to give so much thanks to Mr. Bonenfant. I would not be licensed without him. He took me in as a fifteen-year-old intern, and patiently taught me through every step.

I must also say something about the ethics exam. After reading so much about how it was supposedly no big deal, I went into the exam with the wrong mindset. I didn't study, and thought of it as just a final obstacle to my license. I was wrong to do this.

Of course, with this mindset, I did not pass and had to retake the exam. I want to use this opportunity to encourage other aspiring CPAs to remember to remain faithful and diligent, even in the "less significant" things. Thankfully, I was reminded of the importance of ethics and seriousness of their application in accounting, and again shifted my mentality to one of learning rather than just passing. Take it from me; everything is more fulfilling that way.

HOMESCHOOLING'S GREATEST GIFTS

Memories to Cherish Forever

Mama Vicki

Our decision to homeschool our girls resulted in something so much deeper than young women who are skilled and successful. That one decision forever changed the quality of our lives for the years that we shared together. These girls, and this life, have humbled me, pushed me to do things I never thought I could do and enriched me beyond belief.

Homeschooling has granted our family a quality of life I find amazing. We have had so much freedom—to try new things, to do things together, to make mistakes, to live here and then move there, to serve this person and spend time with that one. It has allowed me to be there for the girls' first this and their funny that. Best of all, we have been able to see, feel and experience this life together.

PRODUCTIVE HOMESCHOOLING

Sometimes when I look through photographs, I am overwhelmed by the richness of our lives. I think to myself, *Surely, I must have lived many times over to have so many blessings stacked up so high!*

Those days spent at home, schooling my girls, were some of the best days of my life. I cherish the memory of hearing the pitter-patter of their little feet as they ran to greet me each morning and the extended morning snuggles I got from each one while I prayed for them individually. I can still hear the sound of their giggles and their sweet high-pitched voices, and the look of their sleepy faces and the way the sun shown on their green-blue eyes and chubby cheeks.

I can still hear the way our girls said "Mama" when they were hurt or in need of comfort from me, and see them all piled on top of their papa, red-hot from wrestling, expressions of glee on their faces. We all loved bath times, as all four girls fit themselves into the tub together and sang childhood songs with soapsuds on their little noses.

Then there were all the times I was able to sneak little glimpses of them when they didn't know their mama was watching—them sitting side by side, or with their arms around each other delighting in being sisters. I would stand at the kitchen window and watch them playing in the backyard, and marvel at their beauty and the immensity of the love I felt for each one of my daughters. Every memory we made is precious to me.

I treasure the multitude of moments we had. We have lived a life of fullness, joy and purpose previously unimaginable to me. I don't know how I can possibly express the depth of what this has meant to me, or how our relationships will be served by sharing history, and sharing life so intimately. Oh, the sweetness of that reality—a treasure I carry in my heart.

THE CESPEDES FAMILY

This is especially meaningful because of my husband's health. He has been struggling with the cancer monster for fifteen years. This cloud hanging over us has helped us to cherish him and this fullness of life even more.

No Regrets

What if the girls had gone to public school? How many minutes, hours, weeks, months and ultimately years would they have missed with their dad and with each other?

What if I had gone to work and chosen a career over this endeavor, especially when we needed the money? What kind of woman would I be? Would I have had five daughters? My eight pregnancies alone would have necessitated at least six years of missed work, off and on.

If I had chosen a career, which pictures in my heart would be missing? I can't even imagine losing one single memory of our homeschooling years. I can't imagine, for example, not having had my morning times with my girls. That is one of my fondest memories of the time I got to spend with them.

I got up before they did each morning so that I could remember the gospel and spend time with Jesus—something absolutely necessary for my soul. I needed to let my heart marinate in the reality of how much Christ loved a sinner like me to have died for me. This always moved my heart to gratitude. It also gave me the motivation to love my family in such a way that I sought to live out the love of Christ before them, shower the love of Christ upon them, and challenge them to love Christ and others before themselves.

This was the great purpose of my life.

PRODUCTIVE HOMESCHOOLING

I wouldn't trade those days for anything—not a successful career of any kind, a life of leisure, more time at the gym or spa, or even just more time "doing me." There is *nothing* I would rather do, if given the chance to choose again.

I cannot think of a more productive, joyful, fulfilling, purposeful, delightful or amazing way to use those years of my life. It was not a chore, boring drudgery, or an overwhelming burden. I am not saying it was always easy but it was doable. Because God had His purposes in mind and His power in action, He always provided the grace needed. In the end, He worked not because of us, but in spite of us, and He did it well.

Dear reader, whatever it is you are doing right now, stop and go to your children. Slow down, take a deep breath and gaze at them. Drink in deeply how amazingly precious they are and how much they matter. When they look back, I promise you, they will not remember every mistake made, every fact learned, every chaotic day. What they *will* remember is how well you loved them, how often you smiled, the tone of your voice, the warmth of your hugs, the sound of your laugh, and the look in your eyes, especially when they make mistakes or feel inept.

It's never too late to love our children better. I know that even as I write this, I am convicted that I need to refocus on this great goal. Our children tend to be remarkably generous in their forgiveness when we confess and acknowledge how we have wronged them, and I believe they root for us as they see us trying to change. No matter what phase of life you are in with your kids, it is never too late. It may not be easy, but it will change lives—yours and your children's.

THE CESPEDES FAMILY

It's never too late to love our children better.

Love only changes things for good. May God bless your family, and whether you homeschool or not, may you have a productive, loving life that glorifies God. "For it is God who is at work in you, both to will and to work for His good pleasure." Philippians 2:13.

A FINAL MESSAGE OF LOVE TO MY DAUGHTERS

My Beautiful Girls,

Our story together is drawing close to its end. When I think back and reflect on all of the wonderful times we spent together, all the fun and challenges that we have experienced throughout our homeschooling journey, I can't help the tears that spring to my eyes. I wish we had more time to create more loving memories. However, I will forever be grateful to the Lord for blessing me with all five of you, my utmost treasures.

  I thank the Lord every day for the gift of sharing our lives together. I can't believe the wonderful privilege it has been to be your daddy from the time you were born up 'til this moment. I am thankful for the wonderful life we have spent together. I wish I had more days to be with you girls. I so much want to turn one of those upcoming grandsons one of you is sure to give me into a dumb jock, a professional athlete!

  I don't want to leave you girls without a few words of reassurance and some significant life truths that I have learned throughout my time on earth, and which I have tried to pour into you girls. I want you to always remember them and hold them close to your heart.

Your Relationship with God... In the midst of all our lives and all we have attained is the question, *"Who is God and how do we relate to Him?"*

I know that you all have a deep love for God and you want to please Him. I've witnessed you all grow in faith, and seeing this is my greatest and deepest joy. Images of Nana reading her baby Bible, Lili memorizing Scripture, Briana singing hymns, Giana tracing creation pictures, and Ellie snuggling with Mama during morning Bible time, and her recitation of voluminous AWANA verses are all sweet, sweet memories.

Certain Scriptures come to my mind when we ask what the Lord requires from us. Simply put, He doesn't require anything other than that we believe and exercise faith in Him (Romans 3:23).

In Matthew 6:33 he urges us to seek first the kingdom of God and His righteousness and by doing so, all other things will be given to us. This Scripture gladdens my heart because it tells us that when you put God first in your lives, He is going to take care of your needs. I know that Jesus has your back.

I am also reminded of Ecclesiastes 3:11 which states, "He has made everything beautiful in its time..." That Scripture is always so real to me when I see you girls; you are all so very beautiful.

Love God with all your heart, soul and strength; love your mama with all your heart, soul, and strength; and love the game with all your heart soul and strength. In the same way that you girls wrapped yourselves around your mama and her homeschool game plan, wrap yourselves around knowing and loving God for the rest of your lives.

Loving God involves having a personal relationship with Him. When you spend time with Him, your love for

Him grows and He becomes so real to you. Take the time to nurture your soul like you do your body. Read the Word. Study the Word. Live the Word! Take the time and expense to surround yourselves with friends, churches, organizations and events that study and exalt the Word of God.

Psalms 119:105 states, "Your word is a lamp to my feet and a light to my path." Let God's Word be a light unto your path as this will help you in all that you do. One of my favorite verses, Hebrews 4:12 states, "For the Word of God is living and active and sharper than any two-edged sword, piercing as far as the division of soul and spirit, of both joints and marrow, and able to judge the thoughts and intentions of the heart." Hold onto the Word of God for your standard of living, thinking, and loving. And let God lead your life in a loving and profound way.

Be the First Sister to Forgive... Watching you girls bond, not just as sisters but as best friends, has been a source of comfort and joy to me. There is no price I could put on this joy that I feel. And as your mama always says, "It makes my heart happy."

I know that as sisters, you will at times encounter differences of opinions or choices. Because of that, you may want to insist on your choices. When such times arise, I implore you to prefer each other. (Superstar Belicia's preference for *Benjamin Button* comes to mind.)

As you grow older together, there may be times when you girls will want to sock each other up, especially when those nerdy boys come into the family. I want you girls to be quick to forgive your differences. Proverbs 17:19 states, "Whoever covers an offense seeks love, but whoever repeats a matter separates sisters." Never hold grudges and always remember that you are sisters.

Listen to Your Mama... I know you have the words of Ephesians 6:1–3 settled in your heart. I remember teaching this Scripture to you girls. It was the first Bible passage that I thought of for you to learn. It teaches us to be "Obedient to your parents in union with the Lord for this is right, to honor your father and your mother—which is the first command with a promise, that it may go well with you, and you may endure a long time on the Earth."

Seeing you girls obey this passage has contributed to the joy and peace that we all experienced in our home. When I think about all of the peace in our home, I can't help but laugh at what me and my sister Elv (Elvie) made our parents go through. It's only now with you girls that am I able to appreciate their patience and love. (I love you, Mom and Dad.) I know that you will continue to show respect and obey your Mama when I am gone as you have obeyed us during your lives, even into young adulthood.

The Importance of Hard Work… You ladies are no strangers to hard work. I have watched you work very hard in your academics. The rigid yet achievable daily routine your mama put you girls through enabled you to achieve all of your academic goals. From when you were in preschool through high school, your mama was always firm when teaching you to never compromise her standards.

In time, we were able to figure out your different talents. As we did, we encouraged you to focus on them with all your might. It has been truly amazing to watch you succeed and excel. And remember, girls, you could only have come this far through hard work. Hence, I encourage you to continue working even harder.

2nd Thessalonians 3:10 simply states that, "You do not work—you do not eat." Keep in mind that all fields of endeavor require hard work in order for you to succeed. This includes your academics, career, relationships, skills development and every other facet of your lives. Thanks to your hard work and dedication, you can look in the mirror and see the results. And they are many.

PRODUCTIVE HOMESCHOOLING

  Nana, you were the youngest certified nursing assistant to complete the program at Pierce College. You led your baby sisters through the local junior college at age fourteen, finished that with straight A's, got accepted to Masters University and USC. And, instead of spending six or seven years getting those degrees, you saved yourself three or four years of time. You ended up with a degree in Nutrigenomics. (I'm still trying to figure out what that is!) As a reward, you got to study for a semester at Oxford and live the European life. And the result of all that difficult academic work has led you to pursue a music career. Your route has been circuitous but the most exciting, no doubt.

  Belicia, you graduated with your Master's Degree and became the youngest CPA in America. What the…? How did you come out so smart? And humble?

  Briana, your high school trek went by so fast, I don't even remember it. Driving you to and from College of the Canyons while you finished your Bachelor's Degree online was comical. And, it was great to witness you putting in all those volunteer hours at the fire station and mayor's office. I sure wish you would have finished law school, girl. You passed first year and put in the work but your heart was for service to your country. I am so proud of you, my Air Force E3 broadcaster! One year of service down already. I hope you see combat soon, sister.

  Giana, you graduated high school at eleven years old. At that time, you were the youngest kid to attend College of the Canyons (COC). What-what! And now, your work in the ASL community is incredibly honorable. Everywhere I go, I ask about your ability and skills and all I ever hear is, "That girl has got it! She is a professional."

  Eliana, our little Ellie, you have boundless support from your sisters and Mama. I know you too will do great things… like be a pro golfer. I'll be watching over all of you as you continue your grand adventures through life.

THE CESPEDES FAMILY

I pray that the Lord blesses each of you richly, far more than He blessed me. The fact that I am sitting here on the beach in Carpinteria as I write this is a testament to the many blessings that have come to our family. Hard work was always at the center of it all.

Vocation above Degree…Some of you are blessed with your mama's brilliant mind and ease in academics. Just like Mama, school work comes very easy for you. Not so with the rest of us. And because of this, we need to be practical in our mindset and measure the activities and endeavors to which we devote ourselves. Many young people are being eaten alive by their pursuit of college and academic degrees, and derailed by a misunderstanding of what a degree can (and cannot) do for them.

Consider us, your parents, as examples. Your mama, who majored in communications and started her doctorate in psychology, wasn't able to finish her degrees or put them to use because Papa got her pregnant. I too, who majored in football but had earned a degree in political science from the University of Oregon, wasn't able to make use of my degree either. Do not go into debt with the aim of getting a degree—unless it is an advanced degree in a field or profession that you have already identified as being in line with your passion.

As you girls know, I have always advocated for having a vocation above getting a degree because a degree does not automatically bring in money. Even the simplest vocation, however, can be built into a business that can provide a desirable lifestyle. And if you work hard enough and are fortunate like your mama and papa, your vocation can be something that blesses many.

Regardless of whether you pursue a degree or not, I advise you to read, read, read. Fill up your minds with knowledge on a variety of topics. Only then can you say that you have had an education.

PRODUCTIVE HOMESCHOOLING

Remember, there are twenty-two million people in Los Angeles in need of services. With a good work ethic, the constant pursuit of knowledge, and a heart for service, you can meet their needs, build your business and reputation and become a professional in constant demand. Your diligence, work ethic, trade knowledge, desire and ability to utilize every opportunity will enrich your capacity to create wealth.

Let Persistence be Your Finest Quality…Hard work alone cannot bring you the desired results. You need a persistent, stubborn attitude. Briana, you are the most stubborn, knuckleheaded girl in the world—and that is all good! As Bill Bradley once said, "Ambition is the path to success, yet persistence is the vehicle that you arrive in." I urge you to keep moving forward with whatever you do. Never park the car.

Enjoy the Rewards of Competition…Never stop competing. It is fun! Competing against yourself and your limitations is the spice of life. Always study. Always learn new things. Always try to improve yourself and your circumstances, as this brings joy and balances out the challenges in life.

Never be afraid to fail big. If you don't fail, you don't learn from your mistakes. So, try. And if you do fail, try harder. Look at me as an example. Daddy has made so many dang errors, I could write a book about them!

The only thing that I disagree with in our conservative Christian movement is the assumption that if you are competitive or ambitious, you are prideful and hence in sin. Experience has taught me that this view is born of ignorance. Even Proverbs 22:29 encourages skillfulness and hard work, and states that such people will stand before kings.

I could have retired years ago in a small house in Los Angeles, kicked back and not given much thought to the future. Then 2008 happened. I realized how difficult life can be at times. That realization led me to remember how important it was to develop competitive advantages to help you progress and overcome life's hurdles. So, I came out of that experience by getting back to work. And I haven't stopped working since. Remain competitive until the end, ladies. Bam!

Seek Wisdom… "The fear of God is the beginning of wisdom, and knowledge of the holy one is understanding." (Proverbs 9:10) If you girls form a relationship with God, you will have a genuine sense of awe for His majesty, His grace and His condemnation. Considering that God is not just a loving creator and father but also a judge, His words must be looked upon as the beginning of wisdom. Get in line, girls, and live accordingly, as we all must.

When You Say I Do… Girls, promise me that you will love your husband faithfully and selflessly. Many young people get married today because of what they can get from it more than what they can *give* their spouses. They are more in love with the idea of marriage than they are in love with their spouses. Always remember—keep God first in your marriage. He will help you love your husband unselfishly and unconditionally and be a blessing to him. Be a woman of gratitude and sweetness that will give him wings to be the best man he can be. The two of you together can honor God as you keep your vows, working through the conflict and difficult days that will come. For they offer you an opportunity for a deeper love and a realization that the hard days are few in comparison to the immeasurable joy and fulfillment found when you seek to relate according to the wisdom God has offered you in His Word.

Be humble, acknowledging your own sin and weaknesses, and love him enough to exhort him when needed and speak truth into his life. Sometimes we husbands can be knuckleheads and need a strong but gentle rebuke. Be sacrificial even when he is not and you will teach him how to love. Shower the hardhearted fellow with your warmth, kindness, mercy and grace and be quick to forgive. This will create a sweet and loving relationship between you two. Strive to be that kind of wife, dears. No man would ever think to leave that kind of wife.

This is how I feel about your mama. What a jewel your mama was when I married her and, like a precious jewel, her value has increased all the more with time. I have no doubt that he who finds a wife has found a good thing, and receives favor from the Lord (Proverbs 18:22). You are a precious gift from God to me. I love you, Vicki.

On the other side, be sacrificial where they are not and you will teach them how to love. Help foster a sweet and loving relationship between you two. Strive to be that kind of wife, dears. No man would ever think to leave that kind of wife.

You girls' love for Mama and each other was due to the obedience we instilled in you. It was like a linking chain to other attributes that you girls possess or can acquire. You may ask, "What attributes, Papa?" Love, joy, peace, patience, kindness and the big one—self-control. These qualities that Mama was devoted to building up in you came about primarily as a product of your obedience. So, make the teaching of obedience a practice in your own home and continue to train up your family and your own heart in this way.

Tell me, "I Love You, Papa."…I enjoy spending time with you girls so very much, as if you were my peers. (If only one of you knew how to swing a golf club, then we would be sports buddies, too.) I am grateful for all of the conversations we've shared, the times we spent playing tennis, wrestling on the carpet, playing on the beach, playing board games, talking about boys, talking business.

I know that you love me so much, just as I love you with all of my heart. But I have one question. Can a brother get some I–love–you's around here, please? I need to hear "I love you, Papa" from you much more as my cancer takes a toll and my inevitable passage date nears. Your whole lives I have tried

THE CESPEDES FAMILY

to be strong for you and Mama, and kept busy trying to help you achieve your goals. Now, I look back and see that I could have said I love you more to you girls.

Maybe it is this journey that I am on that is making me realize that there can never be enough I love you's for us all.

Dying of Cancer… *"Dying is the easy part, it is the living that will kill you."* I heard that somewhere and laughed a great deal at the truth in the statement. I don't mind dying at all. Why? Because I know that Jesus is building me a home that I can work on forever. You ladies know how I like to cut walls and break stuff just to redo it anew. So now I will have an endless construction project to work on, and every moment of it will be as perfect as heaven itself. (At last, some really square edges and my favorite color, forest green, instead of Mama's brown.)

Heaven awaits me, ladies. How glorious a contemplation is that? Think about it. It is an eternal home where there are no tears, no pain, no hunger and no more death or crying or mourning. Just thinking about no longer being in pain makes me ask, "Now, who is the lucky one in this crowd?"

So, stop your mourning and get on with living because I certainly am. R.C. Sproll said it best when he said, "I'm not leaving you guys; I'm just going ahead of you with a new address." John 14:2–3 also reminds me, "My father's house has many rooms; if that were not so, would I have told you that I am going there to prepare a place for you? And if I go and prepare a place for you, I will come back and take you to be with me that you also may be where I am." There you go, ladies. I'm just changing my address.

My ambition my whole life was to make professional, preaching pitchers—but then the five of you amazing girls came along. I decided instead to channel that desire into each of you. You ladies have been the highlight of my life. You have accomplished so much already. Go, girls, and dominate this life!

PRODUCTIVE HOMESCHOOLING

I love you all. Lord bless you. I will see you girls again. When I see you in Heaven, I will build a room for each of you, as long as you don't mind me pounding on the walls with a hammer at six o'clock in the morning. (p.s. Can one of you hurry up and get married so I can make a professional, preaching pitcher out of one of those grandsons, please?)

GREAT QUOTES ABOUT EDUCATION

"A teacher affects eternity; he can never tell where his influence stops."
~ Henry Adams

"It's not what is poured into a student that counts, but what is planted."
~ Linda Conway

"They know enough who know how to learn."
~ Henry Adams

"It's not that I'm so smart, it's just that I stay with problems longer."
~ Albert Einstein

"Learning is not attained by chance; it must be sought for with ardor and attended to with diligence."
~ Abigail Adams

THE CESPEDES FAMILY

"Education is simply the soul of a society as it passes from one generation to another."
~ Gilbert K. Chesterton

"All learning is understanding relationships."
~ George Washington Carver

"Learning is not a spectator sport."
~ Unknown

"Teaching should be such that what is offered is perceived as a valuable gift and not as hard duty."
~ Albert Einstein

"Educating the mind without educating the heart is no education at all."
~ Aristotle

"Teaching kids to count is fine, but teaching them what counts is best."
~ Bob Talbert

"The aim of education should be to teach us rather how to think, than what to think—rather to improve our minds, so as to enable us to think for ourselves, than to load the memory with the thoughts of other men."
~ Bill Beattie

"The only person who is educated is the one who has learned how to learn and change."
~ Carl Rogers

"Of all the joyous motives of school life, the love of knowledge is the only abiding one; the only one which

determines the scale, so to speak, upon which the person will hereafter live."
~ Charlotte Mason

"You can teach a student a lesson for a day; but if you can teach him to learn by creating curiosity, he will continue the learning process as long as he lives."
~ Clay P. Bedford

"Education is soul crafting."
~ Cornel West

"Education is the ability to meet life's situations."
~ Dr. John G. Hibben

"Many highly intelligent people are poor thinkers. Many people of average intelligence are skilled thinkers. The power of a car is separate from the way the car is driven."
~ Edward De Bono

"Example isn't another way to teach, it is the only way to teach."
~ Albert Einstein

"The most important function of education at any level is to develop the personality of the individual and the significance of his life to himself and to others."
~ Grayson L. Kirk

"The supreme end of education is expert discernment in all things—the power to tell the good from the bad, the genuine from the counterfeit, and to prefer the good and the genuine to the bad and the counterfeit."
~ Samuel Johnson

THE CESPEDES FAMILY

"We need to move beyond the idea that an education is something provided for us, and toward the idea that an education is something that we create for ourselves."
~ *Stephen Downes*

RESOURCES

The Home School Legal Defense Association (HSLDA)
HSLDA describes itself on its website as a Christian organization. They are a U.S.-based "nonprofit advocacy organization established to defend and advance the constitutional right of parents to direct the education of their children and to protect family freedoms."

Christian Home Educators Association of California (CHEA)
CHEA holds annual conferences that seek to support and educate families throughout their homeschool journey. It is a huge conference with opportunities to meet hundreds of families and be introduced to thousands of curriculum ideas.

Accelerated Christian Education (ACE)
ACE is an American company which produces the Accelerated Christian Education school curriculum K-12, structured around a literal interpretation of the Bible. It teaches other academic subjects from a protestant fundamentalist or conservative evangelical standpoint. This curriculum can be taught independently or with an umbrella school. It is a good option for anyone living outside the U.S. who wishes to homeschool their kids.

THE CESPEDES FAMILY

Seton Testing Services
Seton Testing Services offers standardized tests, diagnostic tests, supplemental tests and test-prep resources that you can use in your home to help monitor your student's progress.

The American School of Correspondence
The American School of Correspondence is an American distance-education high school in Lansing, Illinois, founded in 1897. It is accredited by the Middle States Association of Colleges and Schools and the National Council for Private School Accreditation. This program allows you to do one subject at a time if you wish and do the courses at your own pace. The school has a long history and strong accreditation so the transcript from this school really carried some weight. It helped us in our local college in terms of getting permission for the girls to enroll, as well as qualifying for FAFSA.

TIPS FOR ASSESSING HOMESCHOOL OPTIONS

There has been a paradigm shift in education with the advent of online and virtual learning. This shift has begun to open up the box of conventional education to include tremendous creativity and flexibility for everyone, especially homeschoolers. The following tips may come in handy when it comes time to think through the maze of options to determine what's right for your family.

- ☞ Be sure to choose accredited schools. Our recommendation is to stick to regionally accredited programs, courses, etc. This is the highest accreditation in our nation and will therefore be accepted by any university or educational institution nationally.
- ☞ High school transcripts are important if your student wishes to pursue college, so consider connecting with an accredited high school that also has a respectably long history.

THE CESPEDES FAMILY

- For colleges, understand the different types of accreditation and which ones are accepted by institutions that you are targeting.
- Attend a few homeschool conventions. Consider attending the Christian Home Educator's Association (CHEA) convention. I attended CHEA conventions on occasion, and others that featured topics I needed help sorting through. Or, sometimes I selected a conference because they had a speaker I wanted to listen to and hopefully engage with, either at the conference or afterward.
- These conferences are loaded with curriculum options galore—but be sure to also take a look at whatever else is out there, always keeping your child's unique profile in mind. See if you can find things that your child might best understand or most enjoy.
- Keep your eye out for a homeschool family that you might want to learn from or model. Ask if you can spend time with them during one of their homeschool days. Consider asking them (or other homeschool families you identify) for one-on-one mentoring.
- Ask questions—lots and lots of them. Talk to many moms and dads on the same homeschool journey. Learn from each other.
- Sift through what other parents share with you and choose what you believe might fit your family. This is especially important if you are leaning on Christ for daily wisdom and devoting these decisions to prayer. Don't feel compelled to try every single thing that other parents may share with you. Just because it worked for them, doesn't mean it's necessarily a fit for you.

PRODUCTIVE HOMESCHOOLING

- ☞ Hire a homeschool consultant. These consultants are typically moms or dads who have completed their homeschool journey and now dedicate themselves to helping others for a fee.
- ☞ Keep it simple. Choose curriculum that is very simple and clear. This has always been my personal preference and I highly recommend this approach. By keeping it simple, you give your child the best chance of being able to understand the curriculum and learn it.
- ☞ There are many fancy curriculums that are beautiful but overly complex, highly detailed, hard to get through, and entail extensive and time-consuming assignments. Reserve the more complex curriculums for use once you've identified in your child a particular aptitude, interest or passion for a subject. That way, they can go deep and wide into a subject that really matters to them.
- ☞ Be in control of your resource rather than letting your resource take control of you. We tried not to give too much power to our textbooks and curriculum.
- ☞ Allow yourself to use all textbooks, curriculum, and resources as tools for learning. You and your child do not have to be a slave to each page of a textbook, for example. I felt free to skip pages if my daughter showed that she got the concept. At times, I started at the back of the book if I wanted to, or just used a chapter or two. I chose whatever best fit the needs and interests of my daughter. Sometimes I decided that we were done with a book halfway through, other times, we used every page. I had the freedom to make those decisions. It took away some of the unnecessary tediousness of school and what seemed like endless repetition

in some subject areas. If my daughter learned it the first time around, we just moved on.

☞ Try to stay a couple of years ahead of where your child is right now. This will entail giving plenty of thought and prayer to the specific goals you'd like your child to attain a couple of years down the line.

☞ For example, you might say to yourself, *By age six, I would like my four-year-old to be a strong reader.* This will launch you into research about reading programs, phonics, and young-reader series, and guide you in finding lots and lots of books you can use to engage with your child.

☞ If you try something and it doesn't work well, try something else! Keep trying until you find something that clicks or helps. No resource is perfect, but some are better than others for your child.

APPENDIX A

Getting a Grip on Homeschool Regulations

The Ninth Amendment makes it clear that regulation of education is not a power delegated to the government. Whether homeschooling for religious, philosophical or secular reasons, parents looking to homeschool their children can find protection in constitutional law.

A large chunk of information in this appendix comes from the Home School Legal Defense Association (HSLDA) website:

- ☞ Link to HSLDA State Laws: https://hslda.org/content/laws/
- ☞ Link to HSLDA California State Laws: https://hslda.org/content/hs101/CA.aspx

THE CESPEDES FAMILY

This is a wonderful resource for any legal questions that you may have before and during your homeschooling journey. Remember, laws and regulations concerning private education/homeschool are not static; they are constantly being modified.

It is also important to note that laws and regulations change from state to state. Please do the research and be aware of the legislation and education regulations in your state. In South Dakota, for example, homeschoolers are required to attend for a length of time equivalent to that of public-school students. Those in Montana, meanwhile, have different hour requirements based on age: 720 hours/year for grades 1 through 3 and 1,080 hours per year for grades 4 through 12 (as found on page 183 of *The Homeschooling Option*).

Our family lived in California during most of our homeschooling years. For anyone looking to homeschool in California, as we did, we have listed below the various private-school statuses as well as general requirements for California homeschoolers. During the years that we lived in Florida and Texas, we had to conform to each state's homeschool laws and regulations.

California Regulations

In the great Golden State, homeschooling is viewed as private-school education. This means that there is pretty minimal regulation and it is much easier to home educate than it is in other states. In most states, private schools are exempt from teacher certification requirements and are free to choose their own curriculum (as found on page 50 of *The Complete Idiot's Guide to Homeschooling*).

The HSLDA lists three legal statuses recognized by the State of California as a homeschool:

- ☞ A home-based private school;
- ☞ A private-school satellite program (PSP); and
- ☞ Instruction from a private tutor.

Under each of these is listed a series of legalities that you will want to research depending on the direction you'd like to go. In this appendix, I will just reiterate the process that we went through.

What We Did

In 2002, we decided to homeschool as a home-based private school. Here is a brief overview of the steps we went through to achieve this, listed and detailed on the HSLDA website.

- ☞ File an annual private affidavit between Oct 1st and 15th.

   — According to California Compulsory Education Law, children ages 6 through 18 are required to attend public school (California Department of Education https://www.cde.ca.gov/sp/ps/affidavit.asp). Students are exempted from the law by the filing of a private affidavit. This can be filled out online with the California Department of Education (https://www.cde.ca.gov/).

THE CESPEDES FAMILY

☞ Maintain an attendance register.

— A record of student participation in course-related sessions needs to be recorded somewhere (https://oit.colorado.edu/tutorial/d2l-creating-attendance-registers). This just proves that you haven't been lollygagging all day long. I will delve a little bit more into the significance of record keeping, as well as provide links to downloadable attendance forms.

☞ Undergo health examinations for school entry.

— The health examinations had to be verified via an official physician Report of Health Examination for School Entry. Each child had to do a separate examination. Make an appointment with your doctor for this examination and bring a copy of the report form, which can be accessed on the Department of Health Services website (www.dhcs.ca.gov/formsandpubs/forms/Forms/ChildMedSvcForms/pm171a(bi).pdf).

☞ Maintain immunization records or personal-beliefs exemption.

— If you do decide to get immunizations for your child, you need to request an immunization record from your primary doctor.
— If you elect to claim a personal-beliefs exemption, you can sign a waiver stating that you reject immunizations for your child based on your convictions.

- ☞ Keep a list of the courses of study that you are using.

  — A course of study will essentially be a list of all state-required courses. We also included the curriculum textbooks and supplemental coursework that we used to satisfy this requirement. While you do need to include a course of study, you are not mandated to include lesson plans or the details of the curriculum in your course study list.

- ☞ Keep the contact information for instructors and their qualifications.

  — For us, the parents listed their degrees and the institutions from which their degrees were received. However, you are not required to have a college degree to homeschool.

A Note on Record-Keeping

The importance of maintaining strong, consistent and well-rounded records cannot be overstated. In case of an investigation concerning your homeschool, having thorough, detailed records of everything, including student participation, curriculum, artwork, homework and test results will strengthen the credibility of your method of education.

Education law for private schools in California designates that each must maintain the following records in their

THE CESPEDES FAMILY

files (as taken from Time4Learning, https://www.time4learning.com/homeschooling/california/laws-requirements.html):

- ☞ A copy of their completed Private School Affidavit (PSA);
- ☞ Attendance records, which can be as simple as a marked calendar;
- ☞ Courses of study offered in your homeschool;
- ☞ Faculty addresses and qualifications. It is left up to the homeschooling parents to determine whether or not they are capable of teaching their own children; and
- ☞ Immunization Records or Waivers.

Essentially, you are keeping a homeschool portfolio, which documents what your child learned, how that was accomplished, what resources were used and how much progress was made. Maintaining accurate records will significantly help when preparing your kids' high-school transcripts for college applications. Though it took several trips to the college advisor and lots of paperwork, we were able to prove to each institution to which we applied that we had a credible education from elementary through high school.

Our portfolio was paper-based, but there are many web-based options as well. We kept items like photo albums, writing samples (book reports, essays, etc.), and awards/certificates in three-ring binders or in Pendaflexes in the file cabinet. (Don't feel compelled to keep all of your kids' work. Just keep samples of their best work and anything that is meaningful to you or them. The point of preserving these work samples is to give an overview of your child's progress.)

PRODUCTIVE HOMESCHOOLING

Resources for Organizing Homeschool Paperwork

It may seem intimidating to keep all of this paperwork organized. With the advent of technology and with some discipline, it will simply become a part of the flow of your school day. Below are links to printable forms targeted at keeping your homeschool portfolio clear and consistent:

- The Homeschool Mom: https://www.thehomeschoolmom.com/free-homeschool-planner/printable-homeschool-planner-pages/
- Thought.Co: https://www.thoughtco.com/homeschool-record-keeping-forms-1833483

There are many resources out there, so we encourage our readers to put in the time, do the research, get comfortable with your state's legislation, fill out your paperwork carefully and thoroughly, be punctual when turning in forms, and get ready for your homeschool adventure!

APPENDIX B

CLEP: An Acronym to Remember

Picture a couple of small eleven-and-twelve-year-old girls sitting nervously across the desk from a junior college counselor. They shift back and forth in their seats as their beautiful mother sweetly and patiently informs the counselor, "Ma'am, they are accredited exams."

With confusion in her eyes, the advisor responds, "I'm sorry, Vicki, but I've never even heard of these exams. What did you say they were again?"

We soon discovered that in our city's local junior college, College of the Canyons, we were the first students to have ever requested college credit from exams.

CLEP was created for people who wanted an inexpensive way to earn college credit, including service members, high school students, college students who cannot afford tuition, adult students, and veterans. Many people, including advisors, counselors, and teachers questioned its validity when we first brought it to them.

Have *you* ever heard of credit by examination? Did you question it the minute you read it? We remember that when we first discovered CLEP, we couldn't believe it was real! We also couldn't believe how simple, cheap and effective it was to progress our education at a more accelerated rate than we could have imagined. We have come to realize that CLEP exams are some of the best-kept secrets of higher education.

Today, CLEP exams are slowly being integrated into junior colleges, universities and online schools. In our travels with CLEP exams, we have discovered effective study programs, testing sites where exams can be taken, and institutions that accept CLEP credits toward college degrees.

Any and all questions related to CLEP exams can be answered at: https://clep.collegeboard.org

Please remember to check this site regularly to keep track of any updates to applying CLEPs in institutions. As stated in Appendix A, regulations are never static and laws are constantly being modified.

College-Level Examination Program (CLEP)

On the home page of the website, we read that CLEP exams cover over 33 subjects and can save a student as much as 100 hours of coursework and over $1,000 in tuition per course (https://clep.collegeboard.org). Almost 3,000 colleges now accept credits by examination.

PRODUCTIVE HOMESCHOOLING

The purpose for CLEP exams is simple: students with knowledge in these courses can test out of those classes in college and receive the normal credit for them as if they had taken the full semester class.

The preparation for taking these exams can come from AP high school classes, online classes, textbooks, non-credit courses, independent study through programs like SpeedyPrep and InstantCert or on-the-job training.

Here are some key CLEP facts from CollegeBoard:

- ☞ Students take CLEP exams on a computer at official CLEP test centers;
- ☞ CLEP exams contain multiple-choice questions;
- ☞ CLEP exams take about 90—120 minutes to complete, depending on the exam subject;
- ☞ CLEP exams are offered year-round at more than 2,000 CLEP test centers across the country;
- ☞ Students receive their CLEP exam scores immediately after completing the exam (except for College Composition); and
- ☞ More than 2,900 U.S. colleges and universities grant credit for CLEP.

CLEP Exam Subjects

There are CLEP exams offered in multiple categories including those listed below. (For a full list of the CLEP exams offered, please check the CollegeBoard website.)

- ☞ Business;

- Composition & literature;
- Foreign languages;
- History & social sciences; and
- Science & mathematics.

The easiest CLEP exam that we found was Analyzing and Interpreting Literature, which offered six credits at the time. Neither Belicia nor Ivana studied for it and yet both scored very high. Most CLEP exams aren't that simple, however, and require hours of preparation. The questions on a CLEP exam are far more in-depth than those in general exams, so the student will need a comprehensive knowledge of the subject in order to pass (Accelerated Distance Learning).

Who Accepts CLEP?

Which institutions accept credit by examination? Progressively, more and more every year. A common misconception with CLEP is that the students cannot transfer the credits they earn to "good" schools. This is patently untrue.

It is important to note that every college accepts a different amount of credits. So, please contact your desired university and schedule an appointment with a counselor who will tell you exactly how many credits you will receive from the exam.

Below is a list of a few regionally recognized colleges that accept CLEP credits:

- Thomas Edison State University

- Texas A&M University
- University of Arizona
- Michigan State University
- University of San Diego
- Purdue University

Each of these schools provides online courses, accepts CLEP credits and is friendly toward other methods of gaining credits. These are name-brand, regionally accredited and recognized schools that span the country. We encourage students to take advantage of these programs to save money and time, and achieve their goals sooner.

How Did We Do It?

Put simply, we gave up our lives for one month. One month only. We had a designated CLEP Room, located in the very back of our six-bedroom hallway. There was a desk, a lamp and a couple of pillows for back support. Belicia was the first to enter the CLEP room. After some serious dedication, she achieved 70 credits in thirty days. Ivana was next and she completed 45 credits in thirty days.

A typical college class lasts one hour, and takes place three times a week for a duration of twelve weeks. That's 36 hours of class lecture time. You can see why we were so motivated. Though it was a brutal month where the girls intentionally gave up normal life for a short period of time, they gained what most college students achieve in four to six semesters. That added up to years saved in time, tuition and sanity.

THE CESPEDES FAMILY

The CLEP exams that we took covered the majority of our general education requirements. We took history, literature, language, science and math CLEPs. Some CLEPs were significantly more difficult than others, while others were unexpectedly easy. Certainly, the hardest were the math and history exams due to the amount of details that we had to memorize. We took an exam every day. Our schedule would go something like this:

- ☞ Wake up at 7am
- ☞ Study until we leave for exam at 10:00 a.m.
- ☞ Take CLEP exam (studied the day before)
- ☞ Home at 12:00 pm
- ☞ Study until dinner at 5:00 p.m.
- ☞ Break for thirty minutes
- ☞ Study until we dropped

MAJOR TIP: bookmark http://www.free-clep-prep.com. It has been the most useful site for our purposes. It lists every CLEP exam, how many credits it is worth and best resources to study for the exam. It also provides practice tests, options for other ways to earn credit, and much more.

Helpful study programs that we found included SpeedyPrep and InstantCert. SpeedyPrep is an online website that is designed to fully prepare the students to pass the exams. In fact, they are so confident, they offer a 100% guarantee the student will pass or their money will be refunded. (The student is paying under $100 per exam, so the risk is small.)

There are three pricing options so that prices are reasonable and membership is kept flexible for subscribers seeking to keep their education costs down (www.speedyprep.com). It is all based on the 'fill in the blank' flashcard-question format and there is a progress bar that lets you know when you've learned enough of the material. InstantCert works in a similar fashion with the flashcards and also has a helpful discussion forum for students to connect virtually.

DSST Exams

DSST Exams are another form of credit by examination. They were specifically created for service men and women who wanted to get their college degrees without the hassle of spending four years in a classroom. They are often offered where CLEPs are offered and cost about the same.

In Summary

We hope that we have given students and parents alike the freedom to open their minds and explore outside the public-education box in which society finds itself. There are many options for gaining credits besides sitting in a classroom for months on end. CLEP exams are some of the most effective and progressively well-known methods to accelerate one's education. The studying required to pass a CLEP exam alone takes stamina, commitment and motivation. But with low-risk programs and resources such as SpeedyPrep in your toolkit, earning credits can be easier than ever.

APPENDIX C

Champions of The Paradigm Shift

Can you say that you have witnessed multiple members of a family under the age of eighteen graduate, all on the same day? In 2014, a few thousand graduates of Thomas Edison State University did just that. They whooped and hollered while one by one, three Cespedes girls all announced their full names as they ceremoniously walked across the stage and received their bachelor's degrees.

The cheers surpassed even those given for the veterans! That was an amazing moment for our family.

All that has been said thus far may seem impossible. Yet, every method discussed in this book has been highly scrutinized, tested for results, and been proven successful. It is our hope that we can assure you that it is simpler than it seems, and that there are institutions out there that recognize the power and legitimacy of accelerated education. Thomas

Edison State University was our greatest champion for our "freelance" education.

Our Champion: Thomas Edison State University

Located in Trenton, New Jersey, Thomas Edison State University is one of the frontrunners in the surge of innovative education happening in America today. The university has been regionally accredited by the Middle States Commission on Higher Education since 1977 (https://en.wikipedia.org/wiki/Thomas_Edison_State_University). It is designed specifically for self-directed adults, who are looking for flexible, excellent and cost-effective alternatives to public education.

According to their website, Thomas Edison State University's flexible learning methods range from online courses (e.g. Straighterline, discussed in Appendix D) and prior learning assessment to credit transfer and credit-bearing exams (CLEP, DSST, ACT, etc.). They offer undergrad (www.tesu.edu/academics/undergrad-programs) and graduate programs, as well as professional certificates tailored to the needs of adults, whether for professional advancement or personal fulfillment (https://www.tesu.edu/about).

You won't believe this number: for out-of-state students, their comprehensive tuition plan amounts to $9,967. Wow! For each of our degrees (with books included), our parents paid just about $11,000. Because of Thomas Edison's accommodating "a lá carte" degree plan, we were able to graduate with our college and postgraduate degrees debt free, in less than half the time it takes most university students!

PRODUCTIVE HOMESCHOOLING

We strongly recommend checking out Thomas Edison to see if it is the right fit for your educational needs and goals. This school provided us with reliable counselors who worked with our family and helped plan out our degrees, credit by credit. We pieced together our bachelor's degrees with community college classes, Straighterline and other online courses, CLEP exams, and TESC university classes.

For the TESC classes, Belicia pursued her accounting degree beginning in 2013 and completed the full program in three semesters. Briana began and graduated in just two semesters. Ivana received her degree in natural sciences in a total of six months.

One of the wonderful aspects of Thomas Edison is that it provides students the flexibility to proceed at your own pace. For our family, that happened to be an accelerated pace. We have always been extremely ambitious and saw the fun in learning and competing to see who would graduate faster.

If you sit down with one of the advisors, whether over the phone, via email or in person, they will help map out a degree plan specifically tailored toward the credits you've already received, the pace and flexibility of your schedule, and your ultimate collegiate goals.

Other Institutions

In Appendix B, we listed a number of universities that currently accept different methods of accelerated education. Here a few more to add to the list:

- ☞ University of Florida

THE CESPEDES FAMILY

- DePaul University
- Florida State University
- Arizona State University
- Drexel University
- University of Kentucky
- Temple University George Mason University
- University of Louisville
- Northern Illinois University
- Colorado State University
- Emerson College

Each of these schools provides online courses, accepts CLEP credits and is friendly towards other methods of gaining credits. These are name-brand, regionally accredited and recognized schools that span the country.

We encourage students to take advantage of these programs to save money and time, and achieve their goals sooner. (If you would like to specifically check to see if your intended college accepts credit by examination, check out the CollegeBoard website (https://clep.collegeboard.org/school-policy-search). Then schedule an appointment with the school counselor to double-check.)

How Much Exam Credit Does My College Accept?

Credit by examination is accepted by almost 3,000 universities across the country. Every institution has a different policy on which credits, and how many, will count toward a student's degree. To be clear, there are three elements of university credit policy that are significant:

1) which CLEP/DSSTs/ACTs, etc. are accepted by the university;
2) the score you need to receive credit; and
3) how many credits are awarded for a particular CLEP exam.

An example would be the Spanish CLEP. Belicia and Ivana both took this exam and got different scores. This wonderful exam allowed up to twelve language credits depending on what the student scored. Naturally, Ivana received the lower score. Belicia scored high enough to receive all twelve credits at the university she applied for, whereas Ivana received only six credits. When Ivana and Belicia applied to universities, they received a different amount of accepted credits for the language portions of their degrees.

An average CLEP exam will award three credits, and a select few will offer six. Some colleges will accept all six credits, whereas others will only take three. Some colleges do not accept certain CLEPs at all.

Besides CLEP exams, there are online courses, DSSTs and ACTs, Excelsior College Examination, prior-learning portfolios, on-the-job training and more. These will be discussed in Appendix D. Don't assume that whatever credit the exam, online courses or portfolio claims to give you will count at the university to which you are applying. Always be sure to check with your advisor to be sure you're maximizing your college credits.

APPENDIX D

What Online Education Has Done for Student Ownership

Remember the funny expression you used to get on your face whenever you heard the term virtual school? It's no wonder that most people looked at us like we were aliens when we told them we went to a cyber academy rather than a brick-and-mortar school!

We received our bachelor's degrees from Thomas Edison State University, 100% online. When that fact was revealed to our fellow student friends, most refused to believe that bachelor's and master's degrees could be received online and be entirely credible. (We usually got the same reaction to our CLEP adventures.)

Well, online curricula are now viewed as a legitimate path to gaining credit in college. Virtual methods of gaining college and post-graduate credits are now the trend. Not only do many schools, like the University of Phoenix for example, now offer full-featured online platforms, entire *schools* like Arizona State University have moved to virtual campuses. They are steadily gaining more popularity because they offer fully accredited courses that count towards a wide variety of degrees. These include unexpected ones like nursing and accounting.

On-Site and Online Schools

According to U.S. News Education (https://www.usnews.com/education/online-education), here is an abbreviated list of schools that offer accredited bachelor's and master's degree programs on-site and online:

- ☞ University of Florida (Gainesville, FL)
- ☞ Arizona State University (Tempe, AZ)
- ☞ Ohio State University (Columbus, OH)
- ☞ Oregon State University (Corvalis, OR)
- ☞ Liberty University (Lynchburg, VA)

There are others, including but not limited to the following:

- ☞ DeVry University
- ☞ University of Phoenix
- ☞ Ashford University
- ☞ Walden University

Ten minutes spent researching the best online schools will give you more than you bargained for.

PRODUCTIVE HOMESCHOOLING

Our Online Method

We will divulge the secret of our online school success in one word: Straighterline. Straighterline is an online platform that combines a $99/month membership fee with guaranteed credit pathways to accredited colleges that save students up to 60% on their degrees (https://www.straighterline.com).

Here are just a handful of the sixty accredited online courses that Straighterline offers:

☞ Business

— Macroeconomics
— Accounting I & II
— Entrepreneurship

☞ Technology

— MTA Certification Training Course
— Introduction to Programming

☞ Health Science

— Anatomy & Physiology I & II
— Pharmacology

☞ Humanities

— American Government
— United States History I & II
— Introduction to Sociology

☞ Social Science

— Cultural Anthropology
— Introduction to Criminal Justice

Other courses offered include those in languages, sciences, mathematics, English and college prep. Because these classes are conveniently self-paced, the student has the ability to give one hundred percent of their focus to their coursework in the privacy and comfort of their home. These credits are also transferrable between schools, like most online courses. Here is the direct link to Straighterline's website with all of the information you would need to get started: https://www.straighterline.com.

And Now, The Financial Reality (The Part You Really Wanted to Know!)

The financial reality of homeschooling your kids? We are so glad you asked!

Imagine telling your kids fifty years ago that they would graduate college with $50,000 in student debt. They would have looked at you like you were an alien! Well, it's all too common these days. Using online programs like Straighterline enabled our family to have four daughters graduate college debt-free. If this isn't the best part about online education, we aren't sure what is.

In many cases, online classes are less than half the cost of regular university classes. University of Florida offers a comprehensive selection of online degrees at the bachelor's, master's and doctoral levels. Admission only requires a 2.0 GPA. Tuition can be as low as $129 per credit; for 120 credits towards a bachelor's degree, that's $15,480 total tuition.

Just to give you some more perspective, at California State University of Northridge (CSUN), the first-year alone costs $16,184, provided that you live off campus. Total tuition for that bachelor's degree at CSUN while living off campus would amount to $64,736. Living on campus nearly doubles the total cost.

By contrast, for an *entire* bachelor's degree, an online student would pay only the cost of one year at CSUN and still save money. That's a $49,000 difference. And, CSUN is considered one of the most affordable universities in Los Angeles. Need we say more?

Why Online School Gives Students Ownership of Their Education

It is evident that online education is cost-efficient, but most courses are also self-paced and transferrable between schools, as long as they are completed within the allotted semester. This flexibility allows the student to study on their terms, and even work a full-time job while studying. The student could also pursue internships while in school and get a head start on her career, rather than trying to stay awake in class like her peers.

The day in 2014 when three of the Cespedes girls—Ivana, Belicia and Briana—received degrees onstage was really special for our family. That would not have been possible without the convenience of online courses. We hope

THE CESPEDES FAMILY

that with a little faith and perseverance, other families can experience similar moments of great pride and excitement. Online education not only gives the student ownership of their school, but of their future. And after all, isn't that what education is all about?

APPENDIX E

Everyone Needs Support

As pioneers in the educational market, homeschoolers are making headway into academic territory that those who grew up in the public-school system might feel uncomfortable attempting to navigate.

We push the educational envelope. We think outside the scholastic box. Still, every trailblazer needs their troops. Every pioneer needs supportive peers around them. We need people alongside us that encourage us to keep exploring and give us practical aid when we need it. Sometimes we need the confidence of others to remind us why we should be confident in ourselves. That's what homeschool support groups are for.

THE CESPEDES FAMILY

Locating Local Homeschool Groups

Please do yourself a favor and become well acquainted with the websites below. These organizations contain valuable resources for your homeschooling journey, from choosing your curriculum to finding homeschool groups purely dedicated to sewing. Both have been aforementioned, but are re-included below:

- ☞ The Homeschool Mom (https://www.thehomeschoolmom.com)
- ☞ Homeschool Legal Defense Association (https://hslda.org/content/)

Here are the links to their pages on finding local homeschool cooperatives or recreational groups:

- ☞ (https://www.thehomeschoolmom.com/homeschooling-in-california/homeschool-organizations-support-groups/)
- ☞ (https://hslda.org/content/orgs/Default.aspx?State=CA&County=LOS+ANGELES)

To give you an immediate understanding of just how many support groups there are in Southern California for homeschoolers, a list of twenty-three organizations, Meetup groups, Facebook groups, homeschool networks, etc. is provided below. These groups cover everything from afterschool programs that provide tutors for certain subjects to planning your child's next play date in the park. Remember: there is always support!

PRODUCTIVE HOMESCHOOLING

Homeschool Support Groups in Los Angeles County

- Beverly Hills Christian Homeschool Support: {https://www.meetup.com/Beverly-Hills-Christian-Homeschooling-Meetup/}
- Christian Home Educators of the Antelope Valley (CHEAV): {https://www.homeschool-life.com/ca/cheav/}
- Excellence in Education: {http://excellenceineducationhomeschooling.com}
- Family Centered Education of Los Angeles: {https://groups.yahoo.com/neo/groups/FaCE-LA/info}
- Great Education Experiences (Gee!): {https://www.meetup.com/gee-southbay/}
- Home4Kids: {https://groups.yahoo.com/neo/groups/home4kids/info}
- Huckleberry Center for Creative Learning: {https://www.hucklearning.org}
- Industry Kids of Burbank: {https://www.meetup.com/Industry-Kids-of-Burbank-a-Homeschool-Group/}
- Long Beach Homeschoolers: {https://www.meetup.com/Longbeachhomeschoolers/}
- Los Angeles Creative Learning Place Homeschool Support {https://www.meetup.com/creativelearningplace/}
- LA Homeschoolers: {https://www.meetup.com/Homeschoolers/}

THE CESPEDES FAMILY

- ☞ LA Teen Christian Homeschoolers: {https://www.meetup.com/latchon/}
- ☞ Malibu Homeschool Meetup: {https://www.meetup.com/Malibu-Homeschoolers-Meetup/}
- ☞ Mandarin Social Adventurers: {https://www.meetup.com/MandarinSocialAdventurers/}
- ☞ Multi-Cultural Homeschool Network: {https://www.facebook.com/MulticulturalHomeschoolingNetwork/}
- ☞ OC Homeschoolers: {https://www.meetup.com/OC-Homeschoolers/}
- ☞ San Fernando Valley Homeschoolers and Hybrid Schoolers: {https://www.meetup.com/San-Fernando-Valley-Homeschooling-and-Hybrid-Schooling/}
- ☞ Santa Clarita Homeschoolers and Hybrid Schoolers: {https://www.meetup.com/Santa-Clarita-Homeschoolers-and-Hybrid-Schoolers/}
- ☞ Santa Monica Wet LA Child Led Learners: {https://groups.yahoo.com/neo/groups/smwla/info}
- ☞ SFV Homeschoolers/Hybrid Schoolers: {https://www.meetup.com/SFV-Homeschooling-Hybrid-Schooling-Meetup/}
- ☞ Sunland-Tujunga-East SFV Homeschoolers and Hybrid Schoolers: {https://www.meetup.com/Sunland-Tujunga-Homeschoolers-and-Hybrid-Schoolers/}
- ☞ TeachPlayLearn: {https://www.meetup.com/TeachPlayLearn/}
- ☞ Westside Cooperative: {https://www.meetup.com/LAHomeschoolers/}

PRODUCTIVE HOMESCHOOLING

Homeschool Clubs for Recreation/Extracurricular

Whether you're looking for extracurricular events with a homeschool support group or want to include your child in activities with other homeschoolers before jumping into a full-time homeschool cooperative, the following clubs are a great option. There are a million opportunities out there and they are easy to find on websites like Meetup.com and TheHomeschoolMom. (Even Pinterest has some great ideas!)

We recommend checking out homeschool events in your area. Research the organizers for these events and contact them about other recreational clubs in your area. Here are some unique clubs that will get you excited about encouraging your child to socialize with other homeschoolers while learning some marketable skills!

- Homeschool Biking Club: {https://www.meetup.com/homeschool-biking-club/}
- Alec's Chess Club for Homeschoolers: {https://www.meetup.com/Alecs-Chess-Club-for-Homeschoolers/}
- Reseda Homeschool Sewing Meetup: {https://www.meetup.com/meetup-group-HNoeBclM/}
- Improv Drop In, Venice: {https://www.meetup.com/Improv-Drop-In-Venice/}
- SoCal Makers and Making Groups: {https://www.meetup.com/So-Cal-Makers-And-Making-Groups/}
- The Art of the Swashbuckler: {https://www.meetup.com/theatricalfencing/}

THE CESPEDES FAMILY

A Special Note on Special Needs

It is pretty clear that kids living with special challenges are not being served appropriately in our public-school systems. Most of us recognize the unique giftedness of special-needs students. And yet, such kids find themselves in an incredibly awkward position when placed in public schools. The special-education environments within the public-school system into which these children are being placed are designed with the best intentions but are highly restrictive and less than optimal when it comes to learning.

Consider this funny contradiction: public-school administrators seek to separate kids that are considered "abnormal." Yet, we homeschoolers follow an abnormal path of education. So, why do these same administrators want to put us in public school so badly?

What's so great about being so-called normal anyway? No matter what the needs of your child, special or not, there are always support groups. In fact, we might suggest that if your child has a learning challenge (as one of our girls did), homeschool may be your saving grace. It will allow you the peace of mind of knowing that your child is in a safe environment where he or she is guaranteed to learn because the person that loves them most is their teacher.

School is often so much more than just intellectual education. In the Cespedes Family, we entered the school of character, morality and principle every day. It is a gift to be able to give that to your gifted child.

There are many homeschool support groups and clubs for special-needs kids in and around the Los Angeles area, including:

PRODUCTIVE HOMESCHOOLING

- ☞ South Bay Spectrum Learning
- ☞ Los Angeles Gifted Homeschoolers
- ☞ Twice Exceptional Advocacy Movement (TEAM)

Each of these groups caters toward children with special needs to provide them with not merely activities and fun, but also access to tutors who can help them get through the tough parts of learning. Special kids certainly need a special kind of attentive education.

APPENDIX F

The Crisis of Choosing Curriculum

One critical component of homeschool education that tends to cause a bit of chaos is curriculum. Most parents new to homeschool see choosing curriculum as an arduous and overwhelming responsibility. It seems that their biggest concern with homeschooling their little ones is making sure they use the "best" curriculum.

They might ask, "Where do I even start to look?" and consequently, "How do I know this curriculum is legitimate?"

Allow us to use a dietary analogy. The most popular meal in Spanish cuisine is a combination of small appetizers called tapas. We were fortunate enough to try many delicious varieties of these foods during our travels.

In America, conversely, meals tend to come in large, sometimes overwhelming portions, and the components that comprise the meal have already been grouped together and put on the plate by the time the meal arrives at your table.

THE CESPEDES FAMILY

(Take salmon, spinach and mashed potatoes, for example.) It is often more expensive to purchase these full meals, and they usually aren't finished. Worst of all, the quality of food generally suffers at American restaurants and we are often left hungry for more very soon afterwards.

Curriculum can be thought of in the same way. There is the meal-already-assembled-and-on-the-plate approach, and there is the a lá carte approach. With the a lá carte approach to choosing curriculum, you can pick and choose dishes from a cafeteria-style menu. You pick the exact items you want on your plate.

With the wealth of resources available when choosing curriculum for their children, parents may feel under pressure to purchase curriculum that appears flashy and prestigious—or, at the end of the spectrum, easy, pre-packaged programs that remove the burden of decision-making and planning.

Remember that it is not only overwhelming for parents to pick curriculum, it can also be overwhelming for children to *do* the curriculum. Mama recognized early on that choosing quality curriculum that was clear and malleable allowed that curriculum to be adaptable to the strengths, weaknesses, interests, passions etc. of each daughter. That is what is important.

Learning Approaches and Styles

When considering what is best for your children, you must first understand the approaches to education and key learning styles that define the way that your children learn. This is key to keeping motivation and progress in your home. The

PRODUCTIVE HOMESCHOOLING

following educational approaches come from an article from the National Home Education Research Institute (https://www.nheri.org/home-school-researcher-parent-perspectives-curriculum-and-homeschooling-approaches/):

- ☞ **Traditional**...Traditional, pre-packaged curriculum shipped ready-to-use style is the most common type of approach to homeschooling.
- ☞ **Unschooling**...This style of curriculum can be defined as one that focuses upon the choices made by the individual learner. Such choices can vary according to learning style and personality type of each student.
- ☞ **Eclectic**...This curriculum style uses a mixed combination of boxed curriculum, homemade curriculum, and/or individualized curriculum. They can operate as borderline unschooling or borderline school-at-home, or anywhere in between and be considered eclectic.
- ☞ **Classical**...The core of classical education is the trivium, a teaching model that seeks to tailor the subject matter to a child's cognitive development. The trivium emphasizes:
  — Concrete thinking and memorization of the facts of the subjects in grade school;
  — Analytical thinking and understanding of the subjects in middle school; and
  — Abstract thinking and articulation of the subjects in high school.

You must also consider learning styles. Conventional school is really heavy on visual learning. If your child is not an auditory or visual learner, they will have a difficult time in school. We would encourage all students to engage in all learning styles so that they are prepared for their college education, as well as real-life situations, which utilize all learning styles. Isn't that what school is supposed to prepare you for?

However, if a child has to endure a particularly challenging subject, it would be wise to have them undergo a program that plays to their strength, so that they can triumph over the difficulty and lessen their fear of it. Choosing curriculum that doesn't highlight your child's strength while learning a difficult subject will give them very little motivation. And, there is nothing more discouraging to a parent than a discouraged student.

In our family, if Mama knew that one of us girls was a visual learner and that particular daughter was struggling with math, then she would draw the steps on a whiteboard, and even use M&M's for multiplication and Hershey's chocolate bars for fractions. She would let us touch them and count them. She would keep lesson times short, and get creative with our learning styles. Our education focused on the important principles that would matter later on, and didn't demand depth unless the basics had become second nature. The focal point of our education was proficiency, not mastery.

What We Did

So, what approach did we, the Cespedes family, take in choosing our curriculum? As you might have guessed, we chose what we like to call the a-la-carte approach. With four little girls accelerating through school at a fast pace, we didn't have the budget to buy pre-packaged programs. We always had a do-it-yourself approach to choosing our curriculum and really thrived with flexibility.

Mama wouldn't necessarily take a book from start to finish. Often, she picked one resource, used pieces of it and put it together with another resource. It was a very fluid method and it worked well for our sharp-witted girls.

Listed below are some of the key curriculum we used throughout the girls' education:

- **Reading/English**—Phonics Pathway, Writing Road to Reading, Abeka Grammar, Excellence in Writing, Spelling Workout, Latin Primer, Children's Classic Series.
- **Math**—Saxon, Math U See, MCP Mathematics, Developmental Math.
- **History**—Story of the World, Living History, Rare Collectors Books.
- **Science**—Good Science, Biology Tutor. (We used college textbooks to learn science, physics, human anatomy.)
- **Humanities**—Music for Little Mozarts, Classically Cursive, Rocket Spanish Drawing with Children, Economics and You, Training Daughters to be Keepers at Home, Teaching Little Fingers to Play, Type It, Atlas with Owl & Mouse maps, Bible at Breakfast, Encyclopedia of Bible Truths for all subjects.

Resources for Finding Curriculum

We have listed below a variety of resources that we used to find curriculum. One of the most valuable was The Christian

THE CESPEDES FAMILY

Home Educators Association, (CHEA), a massive conference in Pasadena, California. There are many large homeschool conventions like it all over the nation. There are also online resources (Internet searches, The Homeschool Mom, even Craigslist's classified ads!), curriculum fairs (e.g. at churches), umbrella schools, and local homeschool groups.

On Homeschool.com's "Top 100 Educational Websites 2018," you will find some of the most popular homeschool curriculum providers, including but not limited to:

- **Homeschool Buyers Co-op**—Largest buyers' club for homeschoolers with significant discounts on award-winning curriculum (Saxon, Explode the Code, Worldly Wise, Britannica).
- **Classical Academic Press**—Focuses on classical education training.
- **Calvert Education**—Homeschool curriculum with flexible program options.
- **GryphonHouse**—Award-winning publisher of developmentally appropriate resource books for parents and teachers.
- **Sonlight**—Preschool through high school literature-based Christian homeschool curriculum.
- **The Great Course Plus**—Offers a subscription-based model with about 6,000 online courses taught by world-class professors.
- **Apologia**—Offers creation-based science and Bible curriculum.
- **Wings to Soar**—Garnered toward dyslexic students and other special-needs students.
- **College Prep Genius**—Great resource for preparing for standardized tests.
- **Khan Academy**—Offers free courses in multiple subjects and plenty of supplemental material.

PRODUCTIVE HOMESCHOOLING

- ☞ **Singapore Math**—Math tutorial program with three-step learning process.
- ☞ **Teaching Textbooks**—Award-winning math curriculum.
- ☞ **Veritas Press**—Provides complete grade-level packages of classical Christian curriculum.
- ☞ **Rosetta Stone**—Learning technology that develops language and literacy.
- ☞ **Classical Conversations**—Classical Christian education.
- ☞ **Barton Reading and Spelling System**—Tutoring system for kids, teens and adults who struggle with reading and writing due to dyslexia.
- ☞ **Freedom Project Academy**—Private, online, classical K-12 Christian school.
- ☞ **Alpha Omega Press**—Leading Christian homeschooling curriculum publisher.
- ☞ **Excel High School**—Accredited online high school.

Don't be overwhelmed by this list! It can be much simpler than it seems. We girls remember how Mom used to take us to garage sales and even thrift stores. Because we had the freedom to choose all the different pieces of our curriculum, we could really find them anywhere.

The goal was our education, not prestige. We would encourage you to use education it for its original purpose: to teach the young the things of life and to remind the old of the joy of learning.

Made in the USA
Columbia, SC
05 July 2021